TESTIM

Mike DeNardo – ex-Merrill Lynch colleague

Chris McGale: Publican, Pugilist, and Punter, brought street-smarts to Merrill Lynch, the City of London's greatest trading desk. Despite terrible injuries, personal loss, and demons that might consume most, Chris caught *lightening in a bottle* and proved that a life backstopped by The Troubles was not to be 'just another *Irish sob story*.'

Chris's sense of humour, tolerance for risk and *joie de vivre* helps to complement the 'no tears' culture of *Liar's Poker*, with the buffoonery of *The Wolf of Wall Street*, to give the reader a more nuanced view of the hilarity on-and-off a trading floor in the 1990's. *The Million Dollar Irishman* is a wonderful read, and, along with the aforementioned-books, I look forward to seeing it on the best seller list and on the shelves of the *Pantheon of Required City Reading* in the years to come.

Terry Melia – Author, *Tales from the Greenhills*

I read this compelling memoir in two sittings. Chris has the gift of natural storytelling in what could have easily morphed into a thrilling novel rather than an amazing life story of incredible highs and lows. Chris takes the reader onto a journey that weaves between childhood illness, The Troubles in Northern Ireland, a career as a high-flying global stockbroker, and a near-death experience.

Early chapters reminded me of Frank McCourt's Pulitzer prize winning *Angela's Ashes* - a memoir detailing the misery and squalor of McCourt's childhood. After further reading *The Million Dollar Irishman*, a theme emerges of a survivor who has come to terms with the ashes of his past and is looking forward to a happier future. The read certainly picked up my spirits!

Connor Daly – Editor, *Northern Slant*

I can't recommend enough *The Million Dollar Irishman; From John Street to Wall Street*. A powerful memoir, from the warring streets of Tyrone, through a near-death car crash, to life in the City of London. Chris's reflections are incredibly honest, thought-provoking, and inspiring. His story of growing up during Northern Ireland's *Troubles*, of personal resilience, career success, and challenges, has lessons for everyone.

Rowan Fortune; Rowan Tree Editing

Memoirs are rarely this good at bringing together a life's shape, its trials, values; its catastrophes and renewals and triumphs. It helps Chris McGale that he has an incredible life story to convey, from his impoverished origins in Northern Ireland, a rise to social heights in the cutthroat milieu of investment, a horrifying calamity and consequent self-reconstruction, this is a life with a very definite sense of trajectory and obstacles, and one lived with agency and depth.

But more than that, the narrative brings the lifeworlds and people encountered into sharp focus, from that of corporate environments to the hardships of being raised in a pub. We are invited to share experiences, not just have them listed out to us; we are given something of what it all felt like, from the worst pains to euphoric joys. This is a compelling book.

Nial Daly - Writer

An elegantly written story of dreams, success, and loss. From the streets of Omagh to The City of London this book was hard to put down. *The Million Dollar Irishman* tells a story of a man who started off life with a difficult time, persevered and took every opportunity despite the setbacks. Quite an inspiring read and one that could become a classic!

Chris McGale lives in London with his wife and four children but grew up with The Troubles in Northern Ireland. He spent fifteen years working in financial markets in Dublin and London, starting at the time of the *Black Monday* Wall Street Crash of 1987 and finishing as one of the top-earning City stockbrokers – earning more than *The Arsenal*. This memoir traces the journey from the warring streets, through a near-death car crash, to burning out in The City.

Chris McGale

The Million Dollar Irishman

From John Street To Wall Street

This edition 2021

First published in Great Britain by
Chris McGale 2021

978-1-5272-8665-8

Typeset by *Your Publishing Solutions*

For Niamh, and our wonderful children, Kate, Joseph, Alice, and Thomas.

CONTENTS

FOREWORD
BY MICKEY HARTE

The Million Dollar Irishman - From John Street to Wall Street is an intriguing tale of a man who through no fault of his own had a non-productive encounter with formal education. Never knowing his father and losing his mum at a young age meant that his greatest learning would happen in 'the school of life.'

Ever the entrepreneur-come-hustler, from an early age Chris McGale acquired the skill of making a few quick pounds. Having grown up in the environs of a pub and in close proximity to betting shops, he was smitten by the gambling bug.

Ultimately, this led him to a high-flying career in the stock market where he attracted salaries commensurate with top professional footballers.

Whilst there were some amazing insights to what for most of us is the fantasy world of stocks and shares, the even more compelling aspect of this memoir is the resilience shown by the author in the face of family friction, a near death experience in a horrific road accident and the rebuilding of a life both physically and mentally.

Anyone who has faced crises in their lives - and who hasn't - will find much consolation in this work.

PROLOGUE

'That which does not kill us, makes us stronger.'
Friedrich Nietzsche

The Humpty Dumpty Man was the name given to me in 1988 by the head of a multi-trauma team of surgeons that operated on me for five hours at a Belfast hospital, putting me back together again.

At twenty-five years of age, a high-speed, head-on collision with an articulated lorry had devastated me physically and mentally.

Had I not been travelling so fast I would have been decapitated.

In a one-in-a-million near-death experience, my life was saved twice that day.

In another one-in-a-million chance my pay ascended from £1 a week as a bookie's runner at my family's Irish pub, Kate's Bar, Omagh, Co. Tyrone, to $1m a year at the American investment bank, Merrill Lynch & Co. Inc.

And then, in what I would later call my George Best moment, I went on sabbatical from Merrill in May 2002 and never went back.

I gave up the one-million-dollar salary and retired to a darkened room to write my life story.

Over the years there have been many incarnations of T*he Million Dollar Irishman*, the story of my life.

Aside from my siblings, I do not know anyone who was an orphaned child and I have grieved at more family funerals than anyone I know.

I never knew my father, John McGale, who died shortly after being diagnosed with cancer not long after my third birthday. Thirteen years my mother's senior, they told Mum he had six months to live but he lasted only two.

My mother, Kate, a midwife who had her first six children at home above the pub, was then five months pregnant with her seventh. Nine years passed before her death from cancer, a few weeks after my twelfth birthday. They gave her six months to live but she lasted nearly two body-shrinking years.

Several versions of this story were written before I properly addressed my feelings towards my next-by-age elder sibling, Paul. I wanted him to be my hero but ended up hating him.

My childhood relationship with him precipitated my boxing career and I was a Tyrone County Champion boxer aged twelve. The noble art gave me the discipline I needed to stay sane and sober.

The animosity between Paul and me rocketed four years after Mum's death when we spent months bedside-by-bedside at a Belfast sanatorium recovering from Tuberculosis.

A year later, aged eighteen, he entered his first alcohol treatment clinic and I went back to school. By then I had spent a decade living with violence in the home and violence on the streets of Northern Ireland.

My vice was gambling. I lived a feral life of betting on horses, 8-ball pool and poker, scheming school and honing the street-skills that would later help shape my City career, first with Smith New Court Plc. and then Merrill.

Life in The City was kind to me, and in 1998 I married Niamh, a beautiful Irish girl in a Versace dress, by the Caribbean Sea.

A few months later, news came of a bomb blast in Omagh town centre. Thirty-one people died, including unborn twins, and hundreds more were injured.

I helped to raise more than £1m for the Omagh Fund and was later nominated by Omagh District Council for the 2002 New Year's Honours List.

Our first child, Kate, arrived in May 2001 and I began to think less harshly of Paul when he sent a handmade card to celebrate her birth.

The bad blood had lasted for two decades.

As Kate's first birthday approached, City life made me worry that I wasn't seeing enough of my baby. Would she too grow up without a father like Paul and me?

At thirty-nine-years of age the stress of The City was taking its toll on my life, and the satisfaction of having done good for the bomb victims was not matched by the grind of my daily war in the stock market.

I had a million-dollar salary, a million-dollar home, a million-dollar wife, and a one-in-a-million baby daughter. I was also winning and losing a million-a-year on horses and spread betting.

I was a star striker, one of the biggest revenue generators at Merrill Lynch & Co. Inc., globally.

But I was not happy.

I had burnt out.

I had become a person I didn't want to be.

Even I didn't like me.

I was an orphan, a lone wolf, not a team player.

I had a personal transfer fee of $5m on my head.

But the crowds no longer cheered when I scored the goals every day of the week.

It was time for my George Best moment.

PART ONE

The Accident

Merrill Lynch/SNC trading floor circa 1995

SNC Lion and Merrill Lynch Bull – Tombstone to mark merger – 1995

CHAPTER ONE

The Too Muches

It was the early hours of December 16, 2003, a few days before my forty-first birthday. Eighteen months earlier, I had walked out of Merrill Lynch's magnificent new headquarters at St Paul's, London, and retired from life in The City.

I left behind my job as a Managing Director of Global Markets and Investment Banking, and Co-Country Manager for Ireland.

I had burnt out, doing too much of what I called 'the too muches'—a never-ending cycle of long days, late nights, booze, gambling, and the need to *win*; a story recounted in my memoir, *The Million Dollar Irishman*.

It was a world in which I might spring to life before my 5.30am alarm clock and say, 'shit, did I lose ten grand on the horses last night?' And I often did. I had a £50,000 credit limit with Victor Chandler whom I knew well, and lost £20,000 on the previous year's Vodafone Derby, a third of what I had won a month before on Rock of Gibraltar in the 2000 Guineas.

Twisting and turning in bed, I fingered the thickening collarbone that was threatening my very existence and recalled the contents of a letter I had received only hours before from my Consultant Orthopaedic Surgeon, Mr Wallace.

Ossified bone spurs were growing in my chest and were threatening to puncture my aorta, my right lung, or my beating heart.

I'd better get up and write, I thought, hoping to finish the story of my life before my life itself was lost. I was by then halfway through the second draft of my life story.

Sleeping soundly beside me was my wonderful wife Niamh, and in the cot beside our bed, Joseph, a golden boy with a shock of fair hair spiking from his head and a smile to light up any room. Seven months before, I had lifted him like Musafa did Simba in the Lion King, like a trophy, when he rushed into the world seconds after Niamh exited a hospital birthing pool.

Normally, when inspired to write late at night I would light up the PC in my study, but was prevented from doing so that night by the presence there on the futon bed of my wandering two-and-a-half-year-old daughter Kate, in the room below her own bedroom.

Instead, I wrote on her drawing book at the kitchen table and drew myself, Picasso-like, on one of the pages, a gift from Daddy to my beautiful, intelligent, sensitive, girl. She had already adorned the world with a new word, 'inglovesit', a term she used to describe something sticky or unsmooth, the texture of which she did not approve.

I opened a bottle of Château Pichon Longueville Comtesse de Lalande, 1985, one of six 'trophies' acquired for a future celebration at a Merrill charity auction a few years before. I needed a trophy at that moment.

Soon it was four am and the last of the fine wine had helped smooth the wrinkles in my thinking.

I'll do whatever it takes, whenever, I had decided. *If it requires life-threatening surgery, I'll do it, tomorrow.*

The uniqueness of my injuries, resulting from a road traffic accident fifteen years before, involving a DAF truck, its 20-ton payload, and my Renault 5 car, meant that there would be no quick fix.

A few weeks later, I appeared at the Hospital of St. John & St. Elizabeth, St. John's Wood, London, before maybe twenty men, who sat around a huge boardroom table in old, musty, brown leather chairs. My consultant had advised that my case would be considered by a panel consisting of some of the UK's foremost orthopaedic and vascular consultants. I felt like I had entered the boardroom of a St. James' gentleman's club.

Jesus, I thought and felt my heart pound, on finding myself before a court of judges who were about to declare on my very mortality.

'Welcome, Chris,' said the Chief Justice beckoning me to sit in one of the club chairs, as the seated gentlemen extended platitudes but gave no indication of the verdict.

'We have been discussing your case,' he continued. 'MRI scans have revealed significant degenerative change, fusion of the scapular and clavicle bones in your right shoulder, and an ossified mass growing on the sternum side of the clavicle. We have also identified a crush fracture of your Thoracic, T8, vertebra. Had it been detected at the time of the crash you would have been required to spend three months on the flat of your back. But now that it has reset itself, there is nothing for us to do. And there's a severed, separated, rib in your upper right side. As we breathe twenty-thousand times a day, there is no opportunity for the two parts to knit together.'

My heart pounded even more. The news was getting worse.

I imagined myself surrounded by a team of surgeons and heard the sound of drills as they sought to extract the life-threatening mass from my chest; a huge T-shaped bone.

'The fused, misaligned, bone mass, is resting against your aorta, but it won't get any worse. Vessel tissue is tough and will never be penetrated by bone rubbing against it. Just don't have a heavy fall on your chest,' he said with a smile.

There was silence as I processed the information, the wise old men smiling on my good fortune.

'It is the best possible outcome,' continued Mr. Wallace, until, finally, a broad smile swept across my face and my body sank into the leather chair.

'You will live. Just don't fall on your chest!' he repeated with verve to resounding laughter around the room.

A further eighteen months would pass before I emerged from my darkened room and returned to City life in the summer of 2005: three years after my 'retirement'.

I was forty-two-years-old, and Niamh and I now had three children: Kate, Joseph, and Alice.

It was time to lay down my pen.

It had been a huge cathartic exercise, but at what cost?

Niamh had married a stockbroker, not a maudlin writer with zero income.

I had written more than one-hundred thousand words but had left behind millions of dollars in salary.

CHAPTER TWO

Apparition

Having gone back to work in London financial markets, not another word of my memoir was written for eight years, until another high-speed journey saw my life literally flash before me.

It was December 30, 2013, and I was driving from Belfast to Dublin on a route I had not taken for over twenty years.

'Where am I?' I asked myself, approaching a road sign on the dual carriageway that now bypassed most towns on the east-coast route. 'Newry, hah!' The place I nearly died.

The Newry bypass cuts through the foothills of the Mourne Mountains, the highest mountain range in Ulster. The majestic peaks of Slieve Gullion loomed before me, its granite face glistening as the road climbed towards Dublin.

I looked over my left shoulder and saw the rooftops of Newry below. It was not a town I knew well. I looked to see if I could see the grounds of the Daisy Hill Hospital complex.

There, an anaesthetist had ventilated me, induced a coma, and saved my life.

The sister of an Omagh best friend had to be relieved of her emergency room duties when they brought me in.

A Belfast-based maxillo-facial surgeon, Mr. Gorman, aided the anaesthetist. He was on day-surgery at the hospital and later told me that without their intervention, I would have died.

Mr. Gorman had arranged for me to be transferred to the Ulster Hospital, Belfast.

Newry was soon behind me as I sped along the road to Dublin, and I fast-approached another set of road-markings, chevrons that separated the dual carriageway from the next slip road—the A1 to Dundalk.

It was on that road that I had crashed, in the townland of Killeen, five miles south of Daisy Hill Hospital.

Should I go there? I thought, and in the same moment dragged my speeding car off to the left, raced across the cats-eye road marking and dashed to avoid the steel crash-bars that divided the two roads. *Jesus, be careful, or you'll be back in Daisy Hill,* I thought.

I was soon in a wilderness of hills and fields and searched for landmarks to be sure that I was following the right path. When it became clear that I was, I felt a tingling in my neck.

There was no other traffic on the old main road to Dublin, just me steadily making my way towards my Waterloo.

Earlier that day, I had travelled seventy miles, west to east, from Omagh to Belfast, for lunch with a business friend.

We had talked about my fiftieth birthday two weeks before, when I lunched in New York with the Wall Street legend, and my old Merrill Lynch boss, Dan Tully. We had been joined by his wife of more than fifty years, Grace, a woman with an elegance defined perfectly by her Christian name.

'We stayed overnight in Manhattan to celebrate with you,' said Dan, raising a vodka-martini to my name. For them, home was Connecticut. It would not be long until his eighty-first birthday.

I had worked at Merrill and a firm it acquired, Smith New Court Plc., for eleven years. Back then he'd tried hard to convince the thirty-nine-year-old me not to give up on Merrill.

I had brought with me a note handwritten in green ink

from the office of Daniel P Tully, Chairman Emeritus, Merrill Lynch & Co. Inc., along with two photographs of Dan and me in the winner's enclosure at Punchestown Racecourse in 1997, which he had sent to me sixteen years before.

'What a wonderful day you arranged for us,' the note began. I had used my contacts with a racecourse executive to roll out the green carpet for an extended Tully clan's visit to Ireland. They had visited the family's ancestral home at Moneygall, a town of 300 people, which straddles County Offaly and County Tipperary, from where Barack Obama's Irish ancestors also hail.

The note was signed *73's Dan*, about which I had been keen to know. 'It's from my early days in back office at Merrill,' he said, 'Western Union wire code where 73s means Kind Regards.'

Dan never forgot where he came from.

'God bless you Chris, call me anytime,' said Dan as we'd parted for what would be the last time.

I smiled at the thought of that enduring friendship.

'Slow down, slow down,' I said out loud, and reached to cut the noise of the CD player.

A song burst into my head and a huge shiver swept over me. I had been playing that song on the day of the crash.

I knew that I would soon cross the brow of the hill that loomed in front and would then be heading downhill towards my nemesis.

I took a pull on the accelerator and looked around. Not much had changed in the rugged terrain since I was last there more than two decades before.

'Jesus,' I swore. Was I about to see it?

'Damn!' I cursed and smiled.

Come on, let me see it, I implored my subconscious, almost giddy with excitement.

'Concentrate, concentrate,' I demanded, and slowed the car further as we went over the top of the hill. I could see the crash-point about 500-metres below and continued towards it at a now sedate pace.

My eyes scanned every hedgerow, every field, and every cranny, trying to prompt my memory.

I looked for the long-gone hole in the hedge that the lorry went through, after gorging me, and searched the road in vain for tyre-marks and surface-scrapes that were still visible when I first returned to that place.

Then I was at the crash scene but felt nothing. The tension had dissipated.

'Fuck, fuck, fuck. Let me see it! Come on, let's do that again,' I told myself.

Not a single vehicle could be seen in either direction as I turned the car and drove back up the hill. The only sound was the song in my head; my heart lifted.

I felt I was close—very close—to reliving the crash scene.

I turned the car once again in the overgrown forecourt of an old house, gritted my teeth and drove back to the top of the hill.

'One more time,' I said, as if I was about to enter the last round of a boxing match.

I hit the accelerator, gripped the steering wheel, and powered down the hill, as the turbocharged car erupted beneath me.

My foot was flat to the boards and the slope of the road propelled the vehicle faster and faster towards my nemesis.

And then it happened. BANG!

'Jesus!' I cried, just as I had done twenty-five years before.

I saw the lorry sweep over me and inflict its wrath: the noise, the anger, the cutting blade.

I braked hard and pulled the car towards the safety of the hard shoulder.

Just as quickly as it had arrived, it was gone.

'That was it, wasn't it?' I asked, 'Yes…fuck, that was it.'

I was left with a single still image of the lights of the lorry's cab climbing onto the bonnet of my car and the memory of the single word that I spoke; 'Jesus!'

'Be careful what you wish for,' I sighed, as I sat in the stationary car; shocked.

Across the road, I saw the entranceway to the elevated home of the Cosgrove family.

I had followed alongside their garden wall on my way back up the hill, just as the lorry driver had done years before.

It was still bereft of the end-of-wall coping stone that the lorry had dislodged before nearly killing me. Time had stood still.

Beneath me I felt the heated leather seats of my Volvo XC90 and realised that I had come to rest in the same spot where, on October 13, 1988, Karen Cosgrove had got into my smoking Renault 5 and saved my life.

'Should I go there?' I asked myself, reasoning that no one would know if I just went on my way.

'Is Fergus in?' I asked the young man who came to the door of the roadside bungalow. I had been slow to climb the steps, after parking next to the ground-floor garage of their split-level home.

Dogs barked everywhere.

'Just a minute,' he said, 'who shall I say is calling?' while all the time trying to calm the tiny dogs that were dancing around his feet.

'Say it's Chris, Chris McGale,' I said, glad when the dogs followed him into the other room.

In my worst post-crash nightmare, four large dogs had bitten and mauled my arms as I lay spread-eagled, trying to fend them off. They left behind a ragged mess of blood and bones, just as the sheared wheel of the lorry had done.

'Is that you Chris?' said the sprightly man who made his

way towards me. It was as if time had stood still for him too.

'Hi Fergus,' I said, as he stretched out a welcoming hand.

'You know I wouldn't have recognised you at all,' he said, beckoning me indoors. 'You've put on a bit of weight.'

'Do you mind if we put the dogs into the other room?' I asked.

'Sure, you're not afraid of tiny dogs? They're only little toys. Come-on ahead,' he said, as I followed him into the living room.

'Do you recognise this gentleman Doreen,' he said to his puzzled wife and continued before she had a chance to answer. 'This is Chris McGale, the man that Karen took out of that smoking car, down on the roadside.'

'I wouldn't have recognised you at all,' she said, 'but you're looking well.'

'Thank you, Doreen. I was very lucky with the injuries, and the broken jaw finally stopped me biting my nails!' I replied to my welcoming hosts, as the dogs accepted my presence.

The goodwill embarrassed me; I had made no contact with the Cosgroves in more than twenty years.

'Eaten bread, soon forgotten,' I thought, recalling the wily words of an old friend.

But I was glad to be there. Glad to be part of the easy-going conversation. Glad to remember that without these people, I would be dead.

Karen was the heroine in my crash story, but her role was largely reduced to the dinner-party comment: 'What do you say to someone who saved your life?'

Most people answer correctly: 'Thank you.'

There is nothing more to say.

'God, it's a miracle that you survived that accident. You were saved by an angel,' said Fergus, 'and my Karen is an angel.'

'Yes, that's for sure,' I agreed.

'You know, I haven't been here since we went to court all those years ago,' I followed, using the plural because Fergus had been my constant companion throughout the trial.

'You were a brave man to go to court,' he offered.

'You know me Fergus,' I said wryly, 'always the gambler.'

'Are you still in the stock market?'

'Yes, in The City.'

'He wheels and deals in stocks and shares Doreen,' said Fergus, amused, 'in the big money business.'

'Gambling maybe, but with other people's money!' I said, happy to keep the banter alive. 'I don't gamble myself anymore. It just got too crazy and I stopped it completely.'

'It's better to be gambling with other people's money, that's for sure. And remind me, how much did they offer you outside that courtroom in Dundalk?' he asked.

'The first offer was £45,000, and the barrister thought he could get £90,000, but I refused it right away. I wanted to see the whites of the lorry driver's eyes.'

'I guess that's about £250,000 in today's money,' I continued after a pause. 'And Karen had a baby boy back then, isn't that right?' I asked, seeking to move the conversation on.

'Yes, he's a young man now, but let her tell you about all that herself,' he replied, while tapping on the telephone handset. 'Hello Karen, Chris McGale is here, and he wants to say hello. Here, Chris, take the phone out there where you can have some quiet,' he said, ushering me into the hallway.

Like everything else that day, it caught me unawares.

'Is that Karen?' I said, with a hesitancy that surprised me.

'Hello Chris, it is really great to hear your voice,' she said in a soft, border-county accent.

'Thank you, Karen, I really owe you so much,' I spluttered. 'I hadn't planned to come here today, it just happened that way, so I thought that I had better stop and say hello. I remember your dad telling me at the time of the court case that he didn't want you to get into the car at all. The engine was smoking. It must have been scary?'

'I was getting up for work at Daisy Hill Hospital when it

happened,' she said.

'At 6.35am,' I interrupted, 'I saw the car in the scrapyard. The clock had stopped at that time.'

'Yes, that's about right,' she said, 'I heard the bang and thought it was another bomb. Like the one that killed the poor family, travelling from Dublin Airport a few months before. We looked out on the road and could only see your car as the lorry had gone way into the far field. I got into the car through the passenger door and you were in the back seat. The first thing I saw was the hole in your arm. I had to open your airways. You were in a bad way,' she faltered.

'And you used the shirts that were hanging in the back to soak up the blood,' I volunteered.

'I held your hand and kept saying, it will be alright, it will be alright.'

'I know, I know,' I said, recalling the moment.

In a dawning realisation, I learned that I was awake after the impact.

The conversation moved on to small talk about our families; I promised to let them all know before my next visit.

But before the call came to an end, there was time for one more reflection.

'You know Chris, it was shocking, the whole thing. I was shaking for hours afterwards. We heard that you had passed you know?'

'Yes, I know, I heard that afterwards, but thank God they were wrong!' I replied with a laugh.

When the call ended, I bade farewell to the Cosgroves and continued my journey to Dublin Airport, where I exchanged the car for a kiss from my wife and daughters, Kate and Alice.

They would continue their Christmas holiday at Niamh's family's dairy farm in County Wexford, where our boys, Joseph and Thomas, had remained to *help* Granddad with milking the hundred-strong herd of cows.

'I had the most amazing experience,' I said to Niamh, 'I'll tell you all about it when you get back.'

'But why aren't you coming back to Wexford, Daddy?' said my eight-year-old, Alice. 'We're all staying up late for the New Year.'

'I have to go to work in London darling, in two days' time, and I don't want to travel up and down that road again,' I answered firmly.

'At least you didn't miss Christmas,' Alice scolded.

Time was short when I emerged from baggage security to the welcome of a wine bar in the airport terminal.

'I'll have a large glass of white wine please,' I said to the bartender.

'And another, with the bill please,' I said shortly afterwards, 'I'm boarding soon.'

'Yes, I'll have a red wine,' I answered, as the cabin crew began the in-flight service.

My broken neck hurt after the long drive. It always hurts, but sometimes more than others; I pressed it hard into the upright seat behind me and settled down to the small bottle of red wine.

It had been quite a day. I couldn't have planned it; it just wouldn't have happened.

Until a few hours earlier I was unsure if I had caused the crash or not. But the events of that day convinced me that I had not.

It was the driver's side of the lorry that had mounted my car's bonnet, coming over me from my right, the unseen driver riding high over my head like some whip-drawn Chariot-master, steering his horses across the oncoming carnage in a Roman coliseum.

In that moment, I saw my car's wreckage at the breaker's yard.

I remembered the one-inch slice that the chariot's wheel

had scalped from my steering wheel's rubber sheath and the inverted-bend that indented the top of its circular steel frame.

I saw the severed seatbelt that had been torn ragged by the cutting blade, which instantaneously lacerated my hand, elbow, skull, face, and rib as it flashed before me.

It permanently separated the rib and punctured my lung and did so with a noise and ferocity that blew out an eardrum, allowing cerebral spinal fluid to seep through its open canal.

I saw the fixed-mass of my work-shirts that had hung freshly pressed in the back of the car, and now stood shaped and hardened in a blood-filled pile.

That pile rested on a pool of blood, which had stained most of the car's back seat.

The scrapyard memories had lain dormant in my consciousness but were now jumping around in my head.

I saw again the image of the chariot coming over me, about to cut through my body as it flew, while the angel's words replayed over and over in my head, and I sank further into the aircraft seat. 'It'll be alright. It'll be alright.' I was sitting in seat 5C on the half-full, year-end flight. I always try to sit in a C seat, an aisle seat, so that my permanently bent elbow doesn't stick into another passenger's ribcage.

I was glad that the seat on my left, 5B, was vacant, as I dried the tears that had begun to slowly slip from my eyes.

I sensed that those sitting nearby could see I was crying and guessed that they would figure that someone close to me had died and would leave me to my grief.

They couldn't know that I was grieving my own near-death.

I took deep breaths, pushed my back hard into the upright seat, and sat with my eyes closed, seeking to regain my composure.

'Are you okay, sir?' asked the flight attendant, breaking the silence.

'Yes, thank you. Can I have another red wine please?'

The song came back into my head as the wine seeped into my veins.

Its tempo soared as my XC90 raced down the Killeen hill.

Inside the pressurised aircraft cabin, I examined the images over-and-over until I saw for the first time, small memory-flashes of the day, twenty-five-years before.

'Jesus!' I had cried when the pain of the chariot's headlights roared onto me.

'Jesus, Jesus,' I repeated quietly, and saw my arms stretched-out in front of me.

Then I saw it all.

A virtual video-clip of my near-death-scene streamed before me like an apparition.

The wheel of the oncoming lorry rose onto my car's engine and on towards me in the driver's seat, with the deafening clattering, scraping, and screeching, of steel on steel.

The noise drowned-out my cries as the rotating blade careered towards me and descended on my steering wheel, turning it as it did so.

In that split second it spun me away from the underside of the oncoming lorry and spared my life. But still it reached to eat me, hurting me in every way imaginable, cutting and gorging through my body.

Then it spat me out and spun me down the Dublin Road, my car screaming and screeching along the tarmacked surface like a half-ton spinning top.

Everything went quiet. There was not a sound, except for my groaning.

Thirty-thousand-feet below the Aer Lingus flight, I lay on my back; my legs were trapped under the dashboard of my car. I could not move.

I was staring at the pinstriped City-shirts that hung, freshly pressed, on a coat-hook in the back.

Blood streamed into my mouth and was swallowed

involuntarily.

I coughed against the flow, and spat it out, only for it to be quickly replaced with more.

Breathe, breathe! I raged, as though my irate boxing trainer was in the car with me.

Fight, fight! Said the voice.

My arms were spread across my chest, as if folded, left on top of right.

I raised my left hand to try to staunch the wound in my jaw.

Blood ran onto my face from the gaping hole cut through the back of my hand.

I stretched the Frankenstein-like left hand towards my City-shirts but could not get hold of a shirttail. My arm fell prone and lifeless onto the car seat.

Blood streamed into my eyes from my forehead and flowed furiously into my mouth and throat from the hole in my jaw.

Panic filled my brain.

My tongue tried frantically to stem the flow, as I choked and coughed and spat the river of blood onto the seat beneath me.

Soon, I would not be able to breathe.

'It'll be alright,' said the angel, 'it'll be alright,' said the voice, as I slumped in the aircraft seat.

'Ladies and gentlemen, we are about to begin our descent into London Heathrow,' advised the voice on the intercom.

The hiss in my left ear, tinnitus, that has been my constant companion since the day of my near-death, was now the only sound in my head.

Mostly I don't hear the compressed-air sound that resulted from my blown-out eardrum, but it was as if someone had switched on a compressor and jammed it in my ear.

Damn, damn, damn, just fucking leave me alone, I objected.

'Welcome to London Heathrow,' said the captain.

CHAPTER THREE

The Humpty Dumpty Man

Twenty-five-years before on October 13, 1988, police had arrived at an Omagh residential estate seeking my sister Noelle, whose contact details had been handwritten on an organ donor card contained in my wallet.

A year before, they had been at her door bringing news of our brother Martin's death.

I administrated his estate.

The coroner described it as 'death by misadventure.'

He had choked while drunk.

He was twenty-seven.

Noelle had parked her car after finishing the school run and heard voices say her name as she moved towards the back entrance of her home.

'Noelle, Noelle, are you Noelle? We need to talk to you,' said the policeman.

'What is it?' she said, having made it as far as her own backyard.

'I'm sorry... I have bad news.'

'What is it?' she asked again.

'Your brother's dead.'

'Which one?' she replied quietly.

'Christopher.'

'He died outside Newry following a head-on collision with

a lorry on the main Belfast to Dublin Road,' he said.

'You are next-of-kin on his donor card. I'm sorry, but you will need to contact the Daisy Hill Hospital in Newry right away.'

I lay still on an Intensive Care Unit (ICU) hospital bed, with a tube in each nostril. One was hooked to a ventilator that provided air to fill my lungs and the other acted as a drain from which nurses could suck excess fluid from my gut.

I would 'sleep with the angels' for eight days, comforted by an induced coma, while my brain tissue settled into a new order and my mutilated body rested.

I was enclosed behind wires that would keep my jaw clamped for another five weeks.

Outside, family and friends pounded the corridors and fretted.

Would I live? Would I walk? Would I talk? Would I ever be the man I was again?

'Chris, Chris, it's okay, it's time to wake up,' said Noelle as I blinked into consciousness.

I looked around the room, piecing everything together. 'Where am I, what happened?'

'You're in the Ulster Hospital in Belfast, you were in a car crash.'

'Were the police involved?' I asked, as I could see a uniformed policeman sitting beside a bed opposite me.

'Yes, you were in a major accident, you ran head-on into a lorry.'

'And they're after me?' I quizzed. But she didn't answer and leant over me to listen closer.

'Why are you leaning over me?' I protested.

'To hear what you say.'

'Why?'

'Because your jaw's broken and it's wired up.'

'And the police are here for me?'

'No, not for you, that's something to do with The Troubles. There's no need to panic.'

'Christopher, Christopher, wake up, we need to change your bed,' the nurses seemed to say, over and over that day, and the next.

Their tone was always firm as they put me through the ritual: moving me in the bed, washing me up and down, raising my arms, changing the sheets, *torturing me*.

I was tired of waking up. The pain in my head and my body was getting worse, and with every 'Christopher, Christopher, wake up' ritual, the rage inside increased.

'It's morphine withdrawal,' said Noelle, 'it makes you very agitated, but it will pass soon.'

'We're going to try to get you out of bed today,' said my Orthopaedic Consultant, who arrived at my bedside just a day after I had woken.

The softly spoken Mr. Macafee was a gentle giant with a shock of white hair, and I was instantly comforted by his presence.

But with these words, I cried in protest.

'No, no, I'm not ready yet. I'm too sore.'

'We have to move you, I'm afraid, before the fluid in your lung starts filling up again,' he said, emphatically.

'Let's see how you get on later this morning,' he said, pulling away from the bed.

I knew that his words were a message for the nurses to begin. But I was ready for them. 'Don't fucking touch me; don't fucking touch me, you bitch!' I spat through the wires, as the chief assailant approached.

'We have to do this, Christopher,' she replied, straightening her back. 'And we are not used to being talked to like that!' she thundered.

'Why won't you just fucking leave me alone? Just fucking

leave me alone!' I screamed through the wires. She bristled and left followed by her female colleague.

It was not long before a male nurse jauntily approached my bed.

'Are you Christopher?' he said cheerily as he checked my nameplate in an exaggerated manner.

I nodded.

'I'm David, one of the ward nurses. What happened to you?' he said almost incredulously.

'Car crash,' I mumbled.

'Jeez, you took a bad hit.'

'Yes,' I replied curtly, determined not to engage in the mental sparring. 'What do you want?'

'Look Christopher, the nurses are only doing their job.'

'I know, but they're fucking killing me.'

'I hear you mate but what about me helping you out of bed?'

'Okay, let's do it,' I said, after a pause, resigned to my fate.

Everything was in a tangle as David and the second nurse got me out of bed. I was no longer attached to a ventilator, but the tubes were still in my nose.

I felt the IV-line that fed me pull on my skin and the stainless-steel right-angled fixator drilled into my right arm weighed heavily as I sought to extract it from the bed linen.

The bedsheets were pulled back and they took me out on the left-hand side of the bed, although I couldn't lean on that hand as three of the five metacarpals had been severed. Its fingertips peeked over the bandages and flickered meekly at my command.

A previously unseen urine bag was detached from the steel-frame bedstead and attached to a portable steel upright that already contained my clear plastic IV-drip bag.

My legs were pulled, feet first, to the side of the bed so that I could stand.

I could see multiple injuries on my right leg: a four-inch,

scab-covered, V-shaped scar on the thigh that was surrounded by a mass of yellow and black bruising; more scaring and bruising across the knee; and a golf-ball-sized wound on the shin below the knee where the skin had been sheared from the bone.

I stood, dressed in a surgical gown, with my head dropped backwards into my shoulders, and grimaced in pain.

The right-angled frame on my right arm felt like a wing as I gently raised it from its socket.

Everyone was congratulating me.

'Well done. I can't believe that you are the same fellow that they brought in here nine days ago,' said the second nurse.

'Where now?' I responded crossly.

'Over to that chair on the other side of the bed,' replied David cheerily.

'Here, let me grab you under the oxter,' he said as he placed both hands around my upper left arm. We moved to his step slowly around the bed with my feet peeling squeakily from the polished vinyl floor towards the chair.

It was a long way down to the chair.

It was a normal soft-backed, easy chair, but I wondered how I was going to get my upright and rigid frame into it.

'Just ease yourself down and let me take your weight,' said David as I navigated the chair.

I pulled my arms together to ensure I didn't bump my steel on the wooden arms, but as David released his supporting grip and I sank further and further into the chair, I roared and roared.

Every muscle in my body was stretched and pulled downwards as my bodyweight sank into the chair, causing excruciating pain.

The soft-backed chair provided no support as my mutilated body stretched down into it, and with every passing moment pain seared through me in a way that I had never known.

'No, no, no,' I roared, through my wired mouth.

My teeth bit hard on the wires, and in a moment of sheer anxiety, I propelled myself out of the chair and landed face down on the bed.

I pressed hard on the right-angled wing beneath me, ground my teeth against the wires, and wailed and wailed and wailed.

'Please, please, it's agony, I can't take any more.'

'It will be better in a minute, you'll see,' said David, as he and the other nurses returned me to the chair and raised the steel sidebars on the bed.

There would be no escape.

I was condemned to the chair.

'Welcome to Ward 19. It's great to see you, mate,' said David the next day.

He greeted me like a long-lost friend and told me enthusiastically about all the good things I could look forward to.

'I can wheel you into the "walk-in" shower, and wash you. And I'll get out my "trusty blade," shave off that beard, and take away some of the scabs.'

'What about the tubes in my nose?' I was still being fed by a drip and was desperately thirsty. 'My throat is really sore from the tubes. Can't I have a drink of water?'

'Sorry, you're "nil-by-mouth" until the tubes come out. You'll have to talk to Mr. Macafee about the tubes, but my guess is that they'll come out soon. Once they're happy that you won't have to go back on the ventilator.'

'You're the new fella,' said Eileen, a night nurse who greeted me cheerily on my first night on the wards. 'You must be tired after ICU, but don't worry, your bed is next to my workstation and I'll be watching you all night long.'

Despite the comforting words, Eileen was soon busy dealing with other patients and I became increasingly agitated.

I couldn't speak loud enough to be properly heard through

the wires. I could feel the two tubes from my nose sitting in my throat like rubber hoses. My mouth and throat were bone dry, but my body was soaking with sweat.

In ICU they would have pulled back the blankets, lifted my robe, showered me with air from a fan and mopped me with cold damp cloths, but Eileen was working alone and I couldn't get her attention for more than a fleeting moment as she moved from bed to bed, administering medicines.

'Please, please, Eileen,' I said every time she passed my bed, 'I need to cool down; the pain is terrible; I need to have an injection.'

Neither of my hands could press the red button on the 'help' buzzer that lay beside me and all the time the agitation continued to build; the sweat continued to pour.

'Now, let's get this plugged in,' said Eileen as she arrived with an electric blow-fan. 'I can give you an injection for the pain, but then I can't give you another for four hours,' she cautioned before administering the intravenous jab. 'I'm sure that it will help you sleep, and you'll feel a lot better in the morning.'

I was tired and sensed that she was right. But I wanted her to stay with me, just mop my brow and stay.

The fan was doing its job, the painkillers would soon kick in and everything would be fine.

But soon, the pain in my head and body was building again. I wanted to cry out, but all that I could do through the wires was sob and wail.

As the minutes turned into hours, I lay drenched in salty sweat that streamed, stingingly, into my eyes. I tried to sweep it away, using the crepe bandage that surrounded the plaster cast that covered two plates in my left forearm.

My mouth and throat were arid, and the tubes in my nose and wires in my jaw were closing in to choke me.

'Please, please give me another injection; please give me another injection.'

By day I was relieved when I woke in the presence of more nurses on the morning shift and electric light in the aisle of the ward.

'Is everything okay, Christopher?' said a day-nurse one day later. 'I heard that you had a better night.'

'Yes, thank you,' I replied, comforted by the morning light.

'We have to change your bed linen, I'm afraid, but we'll be as gentle as possible. We want to have you looking your best for Mr. Macafee's morning rounds. He always wants his patients looking their best,' she repeated soothingly.

'I want to show you off!' said Mr. Macafee, through a smiley face. He was leaning over me as I watched a group of doctors assemble at the bottom of my bed.

'How?' I said.

'Well, if you don't mind, I'd like to show this fine group of young ladies and gentlemen the wonderful work that our team of surgeons did to make you feel better.'

He was whispering so that no one else could hear, as if my verdict would be their surprise. I smiled at the idea that anyone would want to show me off, and even more at the idea that I had been made to feel better.

'Yes, of course,' I said as he instinctively reached to pat flesh on my hands beyond the bandages and contraptions.

I watched as the group of junior doctors formed a circle around the talisman and he spoke in tones so low the words could not be heard above the fan turning steadily behind my head.

After a few emphatic iterations, gesticulations, and inaudible replies, he turned and swept a theatrical arm towards me and declared, 'This is my Humpty Dumpty Man! We had five surgeons operate for five hours, all at the same time. That is one of the unintended consequences of The Troubles, we have some of the best people and facilities in the world to deal with major trauma. There are over 100 micro-stitches in that face, but as you can see, he is still as handsome as ever. His forehead took much of the force of the impact, and the combined force of two fast-moving vehicles will probably have exceeded one-hundred-miles-per-hour. He suffered a compound linear fracture of the frontal lobe, here on the right side. And an associated contusion. That is a one-centimetre-wide stretch of dead brain cells, literally millions of them, running along the line of that scar. The effects will be like that of a small stroke but won't worsen from here. There is also a perforation of the left eardrum out of which there was a loss of Cerebral Spinal Fluid, which was an initial concern for us, but again, the early signs for him are good, and we will repair the hole after he gets over everything else.'

Micro-stitches, scars, stroke, ear perforations, I thought, as the words sank in. *And a more than one-hundred-mile-an-hour impact; Jesus!*

'His jaw is broken and is now being allowed to heal with the help of the wires inserted by the wonderful Peter Ramsey-Baggs. They will be removed in another month or so, and again, he should regain full function from a biting and sound point of view. This fine structure,' he said, pointing to the right-angled frame, 'looks a bit like a television aerial. I constructed it myself!' He lifted it to elaborate.

I winced.

'That pain is because of some rib fractures that will heal in their own time, and the Haemothorax, a puncture of his right lung, which has been successfully drained of blood. We were not able to identify any fractures of the vertebrae. Returning to the aerial,' he said, smiling, 'you can see that we drilled four entry points here, here, here and here and fixed them to this steel frame, to ensure that there is no movement whatsoever around the area of the right elbow, which has been lost; and the base of the Humerus where there was some bone loss. As you can see we also had to elevate this hand, which would otherwise suffer from *wrist drop,* a condition that may or may not persist depending on the extent of the palsy to the Radial nerve at the elbow junction, but we are optimistic.'

Nerve damage sustained around the hole in the elbow meant my right hand was held upright via a hard-plastic contraption attached to my forearm, at the end of which elastic-band satellites looped around each finger and stopped my wrist and fingers from falling.

'The scaffolding will be replaced with a wrist brace once we dismantle the aerial, and one day, hopefully, he will regain full function in the hand.'

How lucky can a man be! I thought. The extent of my mutilation was becoming more apparent, but with every revelation there was hope, even optimism.

Mr. Macafee had moved to the other side of the bed to lecture on the rebuilding of my left arm too.

'Two titanium plates in there,' he said, 'in the Ulna and Radius, inserted through "open reduction." The broken bones had not pierced the skin, so the excellent Mr. Martin McCrory had to do so instead!'

His audience were squeezing for space at the end of my bed as he unwrapped the bandaging around my hand and wrist.

'Now here,' he said, 'is a very fine piece of work done by our esteemed plastic surgeon colleague, Mr. Nick Hart.'

My hand was double its normal size with the fingers spread like they had just been fitted into a padded glove.

'The extensor tendons on metacarpals one, two and three have been severed and sprung, but before they could be reattached the severed metacarpals themselves had to be pieced back together. All in all, it looks good, and in a month or so we will remove the K-wire that has been inserted to keep the bones stable.'

The master's work was nearly done, but, before concluding, he whipped up my gown to reveal a two-inch scar below my belly button, which was the result of an investigation to confirm that there was no internal bleeding.

'Mr. Brian Best made that perfect incision. All he needs now, is time,' he concluded.

'What about the tubes?' I asked, with almost wishful thinking.

Mr. Macafee adopted a studied pose and began to count on his fingers.

'You were in ICU for what, nine days, and this is your third day on the wards?' he asked, as I nodded in agreement. 'Okay then,' said the showman to his crowd, 'let's take out the tubes!'

'You might like to close your eyes,' he said, as he caught hold of one of the tubes with a pair of tweezers and yanked it enough so that he could grab hold of it with the palm of a hand.

I gasped, as the piping separated from skin and water poured from my eyes.

'That's only the start I'm afraid,' he said as he pulled fast on the tube one hand above the other, like he was hoisting a flag.

I buried the back of my head deep into the pillow and bit hard on the wires until all 30cm of brown tubing, the end of which dripped bile, was removed from my stomach and placed in a sick bowl.

'I hope that wasn't too uncomfortable?' said the sympathetic Mr. Macafee.

'No, it's fine,' I replied, 'thank you,' I said, as he prepared to repeat the process in the other nostril.

I was relieved to be able to breathe again through my nose and would no longer be 'nil-by-mouth.' I would now be fed through the gaps in my wired teeth. And, as I would no longer have the contents of my stomach syringed away, I would now graduate to a commode.

'This is my "trusty blade!"' Said the other showman, David,

as he approached my bedside brandishing a wet-shave razor blade. He lathered soap onto a brush over a basin and daubed the foam onto my two-week-old beard.

The track of the blade hurt like hell as he navigated between the cuts, slowly scraping lines through the growth, like tyre tracks in snow.

I could sit in a firm chair beside my bed and was being fed water and puréed food via a huge syringe. The tasty soups and mashed fruit soothed my arid throat and eased the stress of my jaw still locked together by wire ties woven through my teeth.

My bodily functions returned. I could be helped onto a commode but had to be cleaned afterwards due to the problems with my arms and hands.

Life was returning to normal. I watched the same episode of *Neighbours* twice a day on the ward television, as the romance between Jason and Kylie blossomed.

Behind me on a ledge and taped to the horizontal bars of my bed and to the eggshell painted wall, were maybe one hundred get-well cards, the majority of which were mass cards. Everyone seemed to be praying for me, but I never prayed for myself. The thought never entered my head.

I received a humorous card from the Ulster Investment Bank Chief Executive. "Hurry back. We can't function without you," it read, and on the inside, "No one knows what you do!"

What did I do?

I was an investment analyst, advising fund managers on the buying and selling of millions of pounds worth of shares for the pension funds of major Irish corporations and Government-owned institutions.

At twenty-five I was determined my brain would once again get back into gear and that I would return to the investment world. But that enthusiasm was dampened when I spread an

Irish Times newspaper on the bed in front of me and couldn't read it.

I could see and understand the individual words, but my brain could not piece them together for more than a few lines.

One day at a time, I thought. One day at a time.

A day later I was wheeled into the narrow galley-like patients' toilet and left alone.

'How am I going to clean myself?' I ranted when the nurse did not respond after I stuck an elasticated finger onto the wall-mounted red buzzer.

The right-angled frame meant that I couldn't reach behind my back, never mind my backside, and my Frankensteinesque left hand was incapable of penetrating the crevice of my nether regions.

In my frustration, I stood, pulled my pyjama bottoms up to my waist and, for the first time since my crash, moved unaided. I was bare-chested, as no pyjama top could fully cover the aerial, and shuffled along the sticky linoleum floor towards the door.

As I moved slowly forwards, I passed a sink and mirror, and for the first time saw myself.

'Jesus!'

Despite the ravages that I could see in front of my eyes, despite everything I had heard about my injuries during Mr. Macafee's theatrics, I was not prepared for the sight in the mirror.

My head was swollen like an oversized football.

My hair was matted and fixed with hardened blood.

A long, scabbed, scar ran along my forehead and up through my hairline as if I had been slashed by a cutlass.

A scar ran down the side of my right eye so close that I could imagine being blinded.

Freshly shaved scars followed a line down to my jaw.

The stitches that had patched my face together had been

removed while I was still unconscious, but the red lines that the razor had revealed covered my face like a crochet mat; all interweaved with each other.

My neck, chest and upper arms were yellow and black, pocked with scabs and holes as if someone had shot me with a blunderbuss and slashed me with a thousand knives.

My right side was torn from head to foot, scarred, battered, and bruised.

My hands and arms were savaged.

The four pins that had been drilled into my right arm indented the flesh where they pierced the skin, and the fingers on my severed left hand seemed to move even slower than I had previously observed.

The wires that locked my face together stood out in front of my teeth.

Somehow, I had not thought about any of these things.

All the things that I had been able to see in front of me, now looked so much worse than when I had seen them before.

I took a deep breath, raised my head towards Heaven, and saw for the first time a mass of scabs and scarring that ran from my mouth to nearly halfway down my neck.

Had that line continued for another few inches, I would have been beheaded.

Then came a knock on the door.

'Christopher, you're not supposed to be walking on your own,' said the returning nurse.

'But I can't fucking clean my own backside,' I growled as she helped me onto the wheelchair. The cleaning would have to wait.

I lay on top of the bed and closed my eyes in shock.

Despite all the scars, holes, colours, wires and attachments, my mind was fixed on the huge hole in my jaw, and I knew exactly what it meant.

I knew that from this hole in my face, I had almost choked

to death.

'It'll be alright,' said the voice in my head as I unwound on the bed.

I awoke to the sound of familiar voices.

Through the glass panel at the entrance to the ward I could see a group of friends, work colleagues from Dublin. It was Friday October 28, 1988, and my buddies had decamped from our Ulster Investment Bank workplace to visit me.

I had arrived for work in Dublin like a 'duck out of water,' raw and uncultured, but was warmly embraced by the wonderful colleagues now making their way towards me.

I got off the bed and sat straight-backed in the firm leather chair, waiting for the first of them to arrive.

As she did, I watched her faint and drop to the floor. Her fiancée quickly lowered her onto my hospital bed, as the others followed behind.

'Hello Lazarus,' said the next of the group to arrive. He was quickly followed by another wag who said, 'Who's Lazarus, him or her?' pointing to our friend recovering on the bed.

Another called me the Bionic Man. 'Gentlemen, we can rebuild him...' he said. 'You made a great big hole in that hedge,' he followed.

'Don't make me laugh! I'm too sore,' I pleaded.

Later, I laughed for the first time since my accident fifteen days before, when told of what Mark Twain wrote on learning that his obituary had been published in the New York Journal: 'The report of my death was an exaggeration.'

That was true for me too. One dear family friend, who worked as an undertaker's assistant, later joked that he and his boss had been 'halfway up the M1 motorway with a 'wooden overcoat."

In her distress on the day of the crash Noelle had called my office and let slip that she had been told by the police that

I was dead, and then by the hospital that I was alive. That coupled with national radio reports of a fatal road accident on the Belfast to Dublin road, led to an inevitable conclusion. All around Omagh and the Dublin investment community, news spread like wildfire; *Chris McGale is dead*.

PART TWO

Renewal

CHAPTER FOUR

A Fight with the World

My mother was sleeping when I arrived at her bedside. Her hands were crossed on her chest as if she was praying. I thought of her kneeling at Omagh's Sacred Heart Church, as she prayed intensely, while trying to keep order amongst the youngest of us seven children.

We knew never to interrupt the part of mass where she made the sign of the cross on her forehead, then her lips, then her heart. We knew that she was praying for Daddy.

'Who tied my Daddy's hands,' I apparently said, when I barged into my father's wake room two months after my third birthday. His hands were tied with rosary beads—as if he, too, was praying.

I gently squeezed a little finger, and we shared smiles as she stirred. That thin smile saved me. It allowed me to survive every day during those terrible times.

'Hello Christopher,' she said quietly, addressing me with a formality that exaggerated the importance of my arrival at her bedside. I was, after all, her twelve-year-old son.

'Hello Mummy,' I replied, leaning forward to kiss her on the forehead. She reached for the watch on her bedside locker. Her face was brighter that day, and brighter every day in the week since she had been transferred from the nearby Tyrone County Hospital for palliative care at Omagh General.

'You were quick today,' she said.

'I'm always quick, Mummy.'

I had arrived straight from the Christian Brothers' Grammar School at the end of the school day, just as I had every day since she'd left the darkness, and stink, of her bedroom at our house above the pub on John Street.

It was a room from Hell.

She scratched the palm of her hand and smiled, as she always did at the thought that followed. 'There's money coming,' she said, as the smile broadened on her face.

It was just like the old days, when I would sidle up beside her in our back kitchen, after school, as she extracted clothes from the twin tub. There we talked about 'elbow grease' and she showed me how my dad had tied his laces in a double knot, but I never did.

There she told me the story of a stranger who had been attending the monthly fair day on the cow commons, on Gallows Hill behind our premises, where the last man was hanged in Omagh nearyly two-hundred-years before, who queried the measure of whiskey that had been served to him by my father.

After years of rapidly dispensing whiskey-shots in busy Belfast pubs, Dad declined to use a spirit measure when serving drinks and was not amused with the suggestion that he had served a 'short' half-un.

Without blinking an eyelid Dad took up a measure from behind the bar counter and poured the contents of the stranger's glass into it, until it brimmed. He then whipped the excess whiskey left in the glass into the sink, and returned the refilled glass with the quip, 'Well, there's a half-un in it now!'

As one old friend said of Dad, 'he could read you like a tuppenny book.'

'Getting the Guinness right,' was vital to running a successful pub business in those days and the bottling process, where the stout was transferred to bottles, labelled, and corked, was key to that. A weekly Guinness lorry delivered large wooden barrels to the Kevlin Road entry at the back of our house.

Each barrel contained thirty-six gallons of Guinness stout which was filtered and corked into nearly six hundred bottles, the regular order being three barrels a week and fourteen at Christmas; eight thousand half-pint bottles.

Prominent on the wall of the storeroom was a plaque saying, 'The recommended room temperature for storing Guinness is 20C' and we children had the job of regularly moving each maturing bottle around the radiator-warmed storeroom.

When the outside temperature fell to freezing or below, anyone opening the hot-house door ran the risk of being struck by shooting corks as the clashing temperatures caused them to pop to the rattle of a Gatling gun.

When judged ready, the bottles were stacked upright on three shelves that stood in the middle of the bar counter until they were opened by a giant levered-corkscrew and served up fresh with a trademark creamy head.

The stacked bottles continued to be constantly rotated for freshness, with each empty shelf being filled by the contents of the one below, such that the top shelf never emptied. The bottling process required patience and attention to detail and Dad prided himself on bottling 'the best Guinness in town'.

His reward was a thriving business and an inscription writ large on the labels supplied to him from Dublin: Bottled by John McGale, Omagh.

'One day we'll own the whole street,' said Dad, referencing his purchase of the third of the six properties in that terrace block.

The expansion created Omagh's newest lounge-bar, introduced live music and added new rental income from two flats above the acquired property. He also added a new kitchen and upstairs bathroom for his expanding family.

The plan was to have the new lounge completed in time for the busy St. Patrick's Day holiday celebrations on March 17, when the abstinent men let loose on an accepted break from Lent.

It was to be Dad's crowning glory after nearly forty years of hard work, a deserved reward for a man who was born for the pub business. But although he made one assisted journey from the upstairs bedroom to view the progress of the uncompleted lounge, he never saw it finished and died on February 21, 1966.

His passing was followed soon after by that of his beloved corked bottle. Cottage-bottling gave way to regional distribution centres, steel caps replaced corks and the entire bottling store implements, the copper filters and trays, the foot-peddled cork plunger, and all the tools of my father's success, were thrown on the rubbish tip.

Also consigned to the rubbish tip were all the remaining labels bearing the inscription: Bottled by John McGale, Omagh. But I had my pride in Dad, the pub, the Guinness, and all the symbols of that halcyon era.

Everything I did in my early life was measured against how he would view it, even if he wasn't there to see it for himself. We understood that we were the 'McGales of John Street' and Mum made sure of that.

Her eyes were closed again, and she breathed steadily as if she had drifted off to sleep. I looked at her shrunken frame and wondered, again, if I could see that she was getting better.

'Hope against hope,' my brother Paul called it, as he once again defined my thoughts for me.

We knew that she would not get better, but I hoped that she would.

'My boxing trainer says that I have fast hands,' I offered deliberately.

I was about to tell her that I was set to have my first boxing match but was uncertain about her reaction. She knew that I had joined the boxing club, but this was our first conversation about a fight.

'Ahh, Christopher,' she said, once again using my full Christian name in a way that indicated firm words would follow. 'Boxing—weren't you better reared than that? And what about your schooling?' Her grey-blue eyes had firmly opened.

'Every house has to have one gentleman,' Mum always said—by which she meant a doctor or priest.

Her brother Mick, a pharmacist, was the gentleman in her house. In the post-war days before free secondary education, he had graduated from Queen's University, Belfast. Their parents had paid for them both to attend grammar school in Omagh, which involved a daily two-hour round trip by bicycle.

'Education's easy carried,' Mum used to say in the countryside vernacular of her parents, as she extolled the virtues of an academic life. 'You don't pick it up off the street,' was another of her maxims, a saying that implied brains were passed down the line through good breeding, like the speed, stamina, and temperament of thoroughbred racehorses.

'The Glamour Boy,' was the title bestowed on the gentleman in our house; first to Paul and then to me. He was happy to let the mantle pass, as he hated the fuss that went with the expectation of academic success.

'Is this the brilliant boy?' an old lady asked Mum's sister Eileen at a family funeral.

'No, it's him over there,' I said, pointing at my stone-faced brother.

I didn't want the title either.

With the priesthood in mind, in July 1974, I had attended

a weeklong summer camp of the SMA Fathers, an African missionary order that Mum sponsored, at their magnificent seminary at Dromantine, Newry, Co. Down.

It was a vast complex, set in rolling hills that surrounded a tranquil lake, where the religious teachings were complemented by an action-packed sports week, treasure hunts and evening movies in the great hall.

For me, the highlight of the week came on the last day, when West Germany triumphed over Holland in the World Cup Final. I had shared a room with an Omagh boy, whose family had driven us there, and would take us home later that day.

I had always looked forward to receiving the birthday card contained in a little white envelope from the SMA Fathers, but I was never going to be a priest. I just wanted to go home.

A year before, in August 1973, we holidayed at an old manse house Mum had bought for us at Dunfanaghy, Co. Donegal. The house, St Helens, had the same name as the town in England where she had qualified as a midwife twenty-one years before.

That was after a terrible family holiday in Waterford, where I twice wet the bed at a B&B and we had to leave after Mum rowed with the landlady.

The only memory I have of the Dunfanaghy holiday was of lying alone on top of my bed in the seven-bedroom house, listening on a hand-held radio as Tyrone lost heavily to Cork in the All Ireland, Gaelic Football Championship, Semi-Final.

The holiday was two months after her operation, and as the salty sea air did not 'agree' with her, she decided after a few days to return to Omagh.

I left with her, as I did not want to stay with Paul.

'Don't play with him,' was Mum's frayed response as she did her best to cope with running the business and managing the family.

When we got back to Omagh, Mum said that she would be 'delighted if I never saw another soul.' It was the first time in the weeks since the operation that she could be alone to contemplate her fate. As was the norm in those days, the doctors had not given her their prognosis, but her nurse-sister Eileen learned that she had six months to live. With advanced carcinoma in her bowel and secondary tumours in her liver she would, they said, be 'dead by Christmas.'

By then, in the seven years since Dad's death, she had ballooned in weight, nearly doubling to fifteen stone.

We sat contentedly in the living room, with Mum making her way through a pile of books and Reader's Digest magazines. Dickens and David Copperfield were favourites; 'What is before you, is a fight with the world…' wrote Dickens.

We watched television into the late evening and talked about me going to grammar school and her wish that I use my brain in life. She wanted me to go to the professions, if not the priesthood.

We talked more in that week than we had in my lifetime; I had the 'gift' of knowing when to listen, and when to talk; 'just like Mick,' she said.

It was just Mum and me, in front of the television in the living room in John Street, in 'peace and quiet.' At night, I slept with her in the warmth of her double bed and for the ten-year-old me, it was a lovely place to be.

The following year, after my week at Dromantine, and with the rest of the family in Donegal, it was again just Mum and me at home. She had lost several stone in weight. Her hair had thinned to a wisp. A wig hung on a hook near her dressing table, no longer worn.

She spent most days in bed but would come down to the living room in her nightdress to watch television. I slept alone in the attic in my own bed.

Now, back at the hospital, the ferocity of Mum's response was unexpected. I knew in my heart that she didn't want me to box, but in the six months that had passed since my boxing and grammar school education had begun, we had talked little about anything.

Mum didn't know that things were not going well for me. She didn't know if I had any homework, if I had done it, and if I had passed an exam. She was too sick to know.

'And where will the boxing take place?' she said at last. 'And who will take you there?'

'It's okay, Mummy. The trainers will drive us there—I'll be fine.'

'Good goods come in small packages,' she said resignedly.

'Don't worry, Mummy. I'll win.'

A few days later, aged twelve years, and weighing five stone and ten pounds, I joined the ranks of the Tyrone Juvenile boxing champions.

In the absence of other competitors at that age and weight, my opponent and I received byes to the final, and fought a drab, listless duel in a near-empty church hall. We were the Saturday afternoon *hor d'oeuvres* for the real fighting to follow.

That win was enough to see me selected to represent Omagh Boxing Club in a mid-week tournament, at the Silverbirch Hotel a short distance from the hospital.

Mum was having a good day when I visited, insisting I come to the hospital after the fight.

But she wasn't on my mind as I sat panting in the boxing ring's 'Red Corner', with one more one-and-a-half-minute round remaining.

'Are you here to fight or not?' roared my irate boxing trainer. 'Now go out there, and fight with this,' he said thumping his temple with an open hand; a gesture for his much-used mantra, 'box with your brain, not your fists.'

I had been matched with a tall boy from nearby Enniskillen and the size gap made it a mismatch. In the first two rounds, his longer reach meant I couldn't get past his steady jab and I was taking a beating.

But the verbal battering that I had taken in the corner was more painful than the one inflicted in the ring and I sprung off my stool ready to fight.

From the moment the referee said, 'seconds out,' for the start of the third and final round, I chased my opponent around the ring, got inside his long reach and hit him hard as he back-pedalled.

The crowd roared, and their numbers swelled, as men with beers in hand made their way to the vacant ringside seats. When the final bell tolled, strangers reached up to shake my hand and congratulate me. I stood by the ropes, soaked in sweat, awaiting the verdict.

Just when I began to hope that I might have salvaged a win, the MC declared a split decision. By a majority decision of the judges, two judges to one, the winner was in the 'Blue Corner'; my opponent.

'A great fight, Chris,' said one of the event's promoters as I left the ring, 'we would have given you the "boxer of the night" award if you had won.'

It was after eleven pm when I completed the short journey by bike to the hospital. I made my way alone through the empty reception and turned right towards Mum's ward. Her bed was next to the window at the back, on the left-hand side of the eight-bed ward.

In the half-light, I could see some people congregated around her bed, but could not make them out.

I faltered at the sound of raised voices coming from within, one of them was Mum's. Her frantic speech was interspersed with ironic laughs and despairing cries.

I had planned exactly what I wanted to say to her about the fight: 'He was too big for me, but everyone thought that I should have won, I was nearly "boxer of the tournament"—if I'd only had another minute.'

It was all I wanted to say, but I knew from the way the nurse rushed towards me that I would not be allowed to see her.

'What's wrong?' I asked, in a whisper.

'She's not very well,' said the nurse, struggling for the appropriate words.

'Can I go in—just for a minute?'

Then someone said firmly, 'Chris, please go home.'

Hearing my name, Mum called frantically, 'Christopher. Christopher, come here Christopher, come here Christopher…'

I edged back into the corridor and cycled home.

In the months before her death, my mother had become permanently bedbound and suffered bedsores. Not much more than skin and bones, her diet consisted of jars of Heinz baby food, Complan, a powdered vitamin drink, Sanatogen, a tonic water for energy, and milk bottles filled with cold water from the kitchen tap.

Food items were purchased on credit, on a *food-as-you-go* basis, from the next-door grocery store. Mum owned the premises and the family's purchases were to be offset against the rent, but the growing family's food needs now meant that our outgoings always exceeded the weekly rent due.

Clothes were purchased on a *clothes-as-you-go* basis at Barney McAleer's drapery store. It was an Aladdin's cave of jackets, trousers, jumpers, shirts, skirts, and underwear, everything you would need for school, everyday wear, or a family wedding.

No money changed hands until an invoice was sent home with one of the children and another returned with a cheque.

1974 was a bad year for the pub business. With neither our father nor mother there to front it, for a time the pub, and the family upstairs, operated under candlelight because of a politically driven power strike. A Loyalist pub bombing in Belfast, followed by IRA bombs in Birmingham, Guildford and Woolwich pubs, claimed 34 innocents; loyalist car bombs on the streets of Dublin and Monaghan during the two-week Ulster Workers Council strike claimed a further 33, and one-unborn child; and the IRA shot dead Catholic Detective Inspector Peter Flanagan while he sat having a lunchtime pint at a pub near ours in Omagh.

Before she went to hospital, serious people in suits had visited. Dad's elder brother, Patrick, who lived in Omagh, but whom I hardly knew, offered advice, as did her brothers, Mick and Jim, and a young solicitor, Jim Montague, who had offered to be an executor of her will and would later become a pro bono advisor to me.

Should she sell up for the good of the family? Would we end up in the nearby Conneywarren Children's Home, a place she threatened to send an unruly child on our weekly trips to Granny's when we crammed in the back of Aunt Eileen's Morris Minor?

The decision to stay or go was influenced by the reaction of the family when we viewed houses and bungalows in some of Omagh's best residential areas. It was a sullen group that trudged over the property thresholds, knowing that we were doing so only because our mother was dying.

Mum had laid alone in the bedroom above the living room with no more than a transistor radio for company. The curtains in the north-facing, dimly lit room were always either partially or fully drawn, and heat came from a radiator and an electric convector heater that had once stood in Dad's Guinness bottling store.

The room was hot and dark and stank from the smell of

vomit.

The room from Hell.

Above her head at arm's length was an intercom, connected directly to the bar, from which a message would be sent to the staff for help with the chair commode that stood beside her bed.

We children were called to the room when she banged the rubber end of a broken snooker cue on the bedroom floor. Mostly the call was to refill the bottle from the tap or empty the contents of the patterned paper bin that stood by her bed and doubled as a sick bin.

When she was going through a vomiting fit, she lay on her right shoulder, slumped over the side of the bed, wearily retching bile, spit, and wind into the bin, which she could lift from the floor towards her mouth with the fingertips of her outstretched hand.

When the vomiting was over, she would roll onto her back and beckon forward the figure entering the room to clear away the mess.

The brown, Formica-topped coffee table to her side was always littered with discarded tissues, which we swept into the bin on top of its liquid contents to drain the ugly mix into the lavatory.

We then rinsed the bin under the tap in the bath and flushed that into the lavatory too.

Back in the room, we would find her on her back, taking deep, weary breaths, trying to mop the sick from around her mouth with more paper tissues clenched within her frail right hand. She wanted to be left alone to recover.

Carrying a milk bottle freshly filled with water from the kitchen sink, I visited her in that room every night at ten pm on my way to bed. For her, it was an effective curfew and she always asked if I had brushed my teeth.

'They will be with you all your life, so look after them,' she said.

Excess consumption of sugary drinks was already rotting my thirteen-year-old brother Paul's teeth, and he had acquired the nickname Rusty from his grammar school friends.

Days after her hallucinations, while babysitting with friends, the father of one of my co-minders arrived to bring me to the hospital. It was clear, from his kind attempts to steer away from my questions, that Mum was bad.

I arrived at the hospital at eleven pm to a crowd of relatives gathered in a wide circle around Mum's bed. The other beds in the ward were empty, their previous occupants already dead.

Everyone stood in silence looking at Mum. There was not a whisper until I was led down the aisle towards the bed. I looked at the adults and saw their sympathy.

I looked hard at my godfather, Uncle Jim, for a sign. He spoke only to whisper my name, Christopher, but there was nothing more to say.

Mum's sister Eileen and other brothers were there too—Mick, Packie, Francie, and Johnny, as well as Jim's wife Kathleen, Johnny's wife Eileen and Aunt Eileen's husband Seamus, and some of our older cousins.

There was hardly a sound in the room, except the whirl of a fan that cooled the air close to Mum's head. No one was crying; superstition has it that wailing can bring back the soul of a dying person.

I moved between Martin and Paul and stood in silence, watching as the two Eileens, Marie, and Noelle tended to Mum.

After nearly two years of fighting for life, she had lost about ten stone in body mass. She was a shrivelled wreck of skin and bones and was taking her last breaths.

The skin that covered her pronounced cheekbones was

pallid and moist, and the sound of her breathing was barely audible. Her life was ending, and with it her pain.

Throughout every second of the next three hours, my aunts and sisters mopped her down, checked her breathing and leaned across her body to listen for her last breath.

We looked on intently as they checked again and again, and shook their heads, until her last breath came at ten past two on the morning of Saturday, March 8, 1975. She was forty-six-years-old.

The fight was over.

We boys moved outside to the car park where we were each comforted by an elder relative. Martin would always put an arm around me and did so after splitting from the person attempting to comfort him. Often that would be after I had taken a beating from Paul, who never fought with Martin. A few words from him were always enough to end the fight; 'leave him alone', he would say, and with the protection of my older brother I would add, 'yes, just fucking leave me alone.'

It was only after I had my own children that I considered why there was so much trouble between us.

At nearly five, Paul felt our father's loss more than the three-year-old me. Moreover, I was born three days after the arrival of one of the coldest winters in history, The Big Freeze, when temperatures dipped below -20 °C; so cold the Irish Sea froze in places. I concluded that in my consequent closeness to our mother, he felt robbed.

I was twelve, my mother had just died, and the brother I wanted to love me, hated me.

Me, Paul, and Mum –
Paul's First Holy Communion suit, 1968

CHAPTER FIVE

Mother's Day

Around three am, women from the bedside made their way to John Street to prepare for the wake. The blare of vacuum cleaners woke our little sisters Briegie and Joanie, but they were told that the ladies were pretending to be cleaning because the pub was being raided after-hours by the police, and went back to bed with Coke and crisps.

Practicality always came before comfort in our house. The door to the side hallway on Kevlin Road was open all day through the twelve-hour official licensing period, except Sunday when the pub operated incognito after morning and evening mass.

The hallway led to the pub on the right, the living room and kitchen on the left, and straight upstairs to our living accommodation.

Dust and grime was carried into the house by the constant footfall through our living room from the hallway and through the kitchen from the large backyard, until so much had become tangled in the fabric of the living room's brown nylon carpet that it became more practical to lay linoleum on the concrete floor instead.

The lino-covered stairs were cold in winter and dusty in summer. From the landing at the end of the first flight, one could continue straight on to the darts room on the left and the family's bathroom, which was shared by customers on darts evenings, and with the ladies who occupied the pub's snugs, where they could drink discreetly, away from prying eyes. One lady gave me my first nickname: *wuppenny bit*, child-speak for Thrupenny Bit, three pence in old money.

Paul and I shared a double bed in the attic bedroom, a room that also contained a double bed for Briegie and Joanie, and a single bed for Martin. Joanie was a present for Paul's fifth birthday on June 17, 1966, four months after Dad's death.

Paul was now thirteen, Martin fifteen, Noelle sixteen and Marie seventeen. I was twelve. Our little sisters, Briegie and Joanie, were ten and eight.

The room was a twenty-foot-by-ten-foot rectangle, and its floor was covered by some ancient lino that had, over the years, formed into the outline of the floorboards it covered.

There were some equally old floor mats placed either side of the two beds on which Martin Paul and I, and later Briegie, Joanie and I, kneeled with our elder sisters at bedtime, offering our lives to God; *Now I lay thee down to sleep I pray the Lord my soul to keep, if I should die before I wake, I pray the Lord my soul to take.*

Death was a constant companion in our house.

Behind the bedheads were two giant radiators that provided ample heat for the big room. We used nylon bedsheets in the summer and cotton sheets in the winter; I always looked forward to the cotton sheets.

Overhead, the ceiling was padded for insulation, but on a winter's night we could hear the wind and rain lash off the dormer window and roof, while I snuggled up, brother to brother, in a lap position with Paul.

On that bed, I would stretch into a yoga position and bite my toenails hoping my father wasn't really dead. That he had gone to America to his brother and would come back one day to surprise us. I would go to America one day.

I would be a Green Beret, a desire fuelled by the Vietnam-war-like noise of swirling helicopter blades that flew low over our elevated home, past the spires of three adjacent churches, and on to the nearby garrison, St Lucia Barracks.

For years, the crack of bullets from the army rifle range rang around Omagh at church-time every Sunday morning.

One night before my eleventh birthday, while we children slept, IRA snipers fired from a Gallows Hill gable on the soldiers in a sandbagged sentry-post at the rear of the Royal Mail office behind our house.

Later, as the army searched rooftops for the departed gunmen, the noise of the rotor blades and engines brought us rapidly to our dormered bedroom window, before a spotlight from the hovering helicopter lit up every inch of our bedroom like a lightning flash, and we dived to the ground for cover.

Our house was a mini shrine to John F. Kennedy and Pope Paul VI, who looked down from the walls of our huge sitting room above the pub, and from our parents' bedroom.

On a dado rail were a handful of photographs from our parents' wedding in Dublin and their Clarence Hotel, Liffey-side, reception, a wedding blessing from Pope Paul, a picture of the Pope himself, a picture of their firstborn Marie as a baby, a boxed statue of Our Lady of Grace, a framed memorial picture of JFK, and a picture of our parents in Washington DC at JFK's Arlington Memorial Cemetery graveside, from the time they had visited Dad's brother Felix in Philadelphia in the summer of 1964.

All the sitting room photographs and symbols of my parents' union were later joined by a £1, plastic-framed portrait of the *Mona Lisa* that I had bought as a Christmas present for Mum.

Less than nine hours after we had watched her take her last breath, a line of bumper-to-bumper cars formed a motorcade and followed the hearse from the morgue to John Street.

Soon she lay in an open-topped coffin in the room from Hell.

What was left of her hair was swept back from her head. A pink silk shroud, emblazoned by the figure of Our Lady of Grace, covered her body. Her hands were wrapped in rosary beads that protruded from the shroud, the twisted pearl beads highlighting the whites of her fingernails. On top of the gown would soon lay hundreds of Mass cards left by mourners.

People like to say how happy a corpse looks. One old friend said she looked just as she did as a schoolgirl, thirty years before—the girl at the Loreto Convent Grammar School, Kathleen O'Kane.

It did not seem like that to me.

Placed around her bedroom were freestanding pub stools with black legs and brown leather-padded cushions. Relatives and men from the pub occupied the stools day and night. Many had performed the same duty for my father—a guard of honour in her last hours on the premises.

As is the tradition at Irish wakes, the men were light-hearted. Mum's brother, Johnny, regaled the sitters with anecdotes. I sat late into the night listening to their reminiscences and banter. How she would have loved to be part of it.

Mum's wish was that the wake would be short, and so she was removed after one night at home, to the Sacred Heart Church.

On the morning of the funeral, Granny O'Kane, our only surviving grandparent, was helped through the kitchen door. She was too frail to visit Mum's deathbed, or her wake, and I had never seen her at our house before.

Granny lived on the farm with two of her unmarried sons, Packie and Francie, while Mick visited most Saturday evenings from Belfast.

A few years before, The Troubles meant Martin and I spent the whole summers of 1970 and 1971 on the farm. Martin loved being there and helped the workingmen with their daily routine of milking, feeding, and bedding the farm's dairy herd.

Cassie Kane, as Granny was affectionately known, always had a smile and an easy way, and nothing pleased Mum more than the weekly visits to her birthplace.

Granny prepared breakfast, lunch and dinner for the men, including Martin, cut chunks of bread from an unsliced loaf, and boiled eggs in a blackened baked beans tin on a gas stove.

One of my jobs was to collect the free-range eggs from the chicken coop, and I looked forward to my 'pay' at the end of the summer's work.

To fill the days I roamed the fields, jumped burns, and skipped through reeds and rushes, my rifle-pole held tight as if I was a lone soldier on foot patrol, like the ones now patrolling the streets of Omagh. One day I came across real soldiers on manoeuvres across the same fields. At first the armed soldier next to their jeep was happy for the seven-year-old me to look inside at the two green padded benches, and to examine from a safe distance his Self-Loading Rifle (SLR), before a blast of Roger-Tango, Oscar-Mike, and Lima-Charlie on his military radio changed the cheery exchange.

'On your way lad,' said the friendly squaddie, firmly, in an English accent that I was hearing for the first time.

The annual highlight of those summers was 'getting in the hay', when all my uncles and male cousins would come from their own farms to help with the harvest.

When all the work was done, Uncle Jim sat at the head of Granny's table and congratulated everyone on their hard work, including me. Martin, who had spent the summer doing real work on the farm, sat beside him. We were proud to be part of the family.

Before the coffin lid had been closed, we had stood by Mum's bed and prayed with the mourners who crammed into the landing and stairwell outside her bedroom and recited decades of the rosary for the repose of her soul, over and over.

Then, a hand-made card from Briegie, and a purple pincushion also made at school by Joanie and embroidered in white thread by Noelle with the word *Mum*, had been placed inside the coffin. 'To Mummy,' the card said. It was Sunday, March 9, 1975—Mother's Day.

CHAPTER SIX

The Beating

On my return to school, I was called to see the headmaster, Brother O'Shea, who passed me his condolences. He was a tall, thin, man of about 65 years, with a mane of white hair and a sympathetic face.

He said I should not hesitate to come to him if there was anything I needed, and he encouraged me to work hard at my studies. The briefing was short, and Paul received similar enlightenment. It was also the last time anyone at the school discussed Mum's death with us.

I was relieved that he had said nothing about my poor academic performance.

I had gone from first to last in the class.

I had been a model student. At the end of every primary school year I had been a recipient of awards for constant attendance and I'd had no doubt I would pass the 11 Plus exam and graduate to join Paul at the grammar school.

Now, I struggled in virtually all subjects.

Although I had transferred from the Christian Brothers, Primary School, to the nearby Christian Brothers, Grammar School, and the brothers lived and dined together, nothing was said about my falling standards and no account was taken of my home circumstances.

I hated grammar school.

My schoolmaster in primary school years five and six, when I was aged ten and eleven, was Noel O'Reilly, a Christian Brother who in the spirit of the faith had given over his life to the church and the education of boys.

A 'true-blue' Dubliner, he regaled us with renditions of *Poor Auld Dicey Reilly* and *Molly Malone*. We danced the *hopak*, sang *la cucaracha*, and stayed on the school premises at the end of the day to play chess, draughts, and Scrabble, and to study 11 Plus practice papers.

I stayed with Brother O'Reilly at every opportunity and became his chief salesman and runner to the Cash and Carry when he established a tuck shop for the year six students. There I bought stocks of fizzy drinks, crisps, chocolate bars and biscuits, or whatever else I judged would sell.

With the physical stature of *The Thorn Birds*' Father Ralph de Bricassart, he dressed entirely in black, either in a suit, with or without a white dog collar, or in his fearsome cassock. The mere sight of a raised Brother O'Reilly eyebrow could put the fear of God into a boy.

'Maintenant garcon,' he would demand, light-heartedly. His remonstrations were usually laced with humour, as was his promise that there would be 'wigs on the green'. Similarly, his retort to any excuse was, 'I'd believe you, but thousands wouldn't.'

But as was the norm, he administered corporal punishment to us all by means of a leather lead-filled strap—a terrifying event.

He raged at me after I was spat upon when walking with my classmates back to our part of town from Omagh's swimming pool.

'Fenian bastards,' said the perpetrator, who used a pejorative word that along with *Taig* is sometimes used to describe Irish Catholics.

'I told you not to fall behind,' he said, while wiping with a handkerchief the offending slime from my jacket, after I rushed to catch up with him at the front of the group.

But he relented to my desire to watch the 1973 Epsom Derby with classmates from the assembly hall floor, so that I would not delay Year 5 after school drama group rehearsals.

A fluent Irish speaker, he taught us basic Irish and prepared manuscripts for us phonetically, so that we all sounded like Gaelic scholars. At our first attempt, we reached the Ulster Final of the Irish Schools Drama competition and later staged the play to a full house at the annual Gaelic cultural event, Fheis Tir Eoghain, at Omagh's Town Hall.

He also made or borrowed all the costumes, stage props and the set itself. As we had no school bus, I was one of a group of boys nominated to help him ferry the gear from the school to the theatre.

We did so with a remnant of the town's old railway line, a four-foot-by-ten, flat-backed wheelbarrow, to which we strapped the gear under a red velvet curtain that would later be used as a prop in the show. We set off, pushing and pulling the load up Castle Street towards the Courthouse and then halfway down High Street towards the Town Hall.

Going down the Courthouse hill was like a scene from a *Just William* adventure story; with us zigzagging the steep decline, desperately trying to stop the heavily laden barrow careering away with Brother O'Reilly and us all. There was relief when we straightened the trolley to face the Town Hall doorway.

In the play, I had a role as one of six boys locked in a haunted house. One scene involved a candle moving along a table, unaided, directed discreetly from under the table by a schoolmate.

In another scene, the lead actor shrieked when he noticed the face in a portrait change as other boys swapped places behind the picture frame to make it happen. The play attracted hoots of laughter from the audience, and we took our bow to a roar of approval from the 200 seats in front.

One year later, in the spring of 1974, we were crowned All-Ireland Champions at the finals of the Irish Schools Drama competition at Dublin's Player Wills Theatre, where we had received a commendation with the Haunted House play the year before.

Appropriately, our play was about the raucous activities of a group of pirates and was an elaborate production. We wore bandanas, eye patches, boot polish, painted faces and homemade wooden cutlasses, which we had sprayed with silver paint on a newspaper-covered classroom floor. We made everything ourselves under the watchful eye of Brother O'Reilly.

'Yo-ho-ho and a bottle of rum,' we declared, as we bounced around the stage of the Dublin theatre and in front of the crowds at Omagh Town Hall, at the *Fheis Tir Eoghain*. But there would be no *Fheis Tir Eoghain* at the Town Hall in the summer of 1975, as a loyalist bomb had in the winter months blasted a hole through its front.

At the Christian Brothers Grammar School, there was only one boy from my primary school class among the thirty-strong group that formed 1C (Year 7). The rest came from the townlands and villages that surrounded Omagh: Ballygawley, Beragh, Carrickmore, Dromore, Drumquin, Drumragh, Fintona, Gortin, Killyclogher, and Loughmacrory; boys we townies, or *Omey Gomeys*, disparagingly called *Culchies*.

My first ever lesson at the school was Latin, taught by the lay teacher Vice Principal. Like Brother O'Reilly, he was a giant man with a crop of greying hair who quietly shuffled around the room with his hands clasped behind his back, making an intermittent cough-like noise that sounded like *ahinsp*, quizzing each boy about himself, and declaring some of us to be a 'grey man'.

Had he called me *tran* (colloquial for being a *trying* child), *a ganch, hallion* or *latchico*, I would have understood the insult. But I knew *grey* to have a pejorative context and later learned that it is derived from the Irish word magairlí, which in Gaelic means testicles.

'Christopher McGale, sir,' I said, as he leaned his large frame towards me, examining me closely from beneath his bushy eyebrows.

'Are you a brother of that fellow in Year 9?' he asked.

'Yes,' I said. 'Paul.'

My reply caused a sharp intake of breath.

'No, I meant the other fellow. Barry?'

'He's my cousin, sir,' I offered, hoping that that answer would please him more.

'Then I hope you'll pay more attention to your studies than your brother,' he groaned, and moved along to the next boy.

But it was the message that followed about notes, files, routine, and setting aside two hours' study time every single evening, that horrified me. I knew that there was no way that I was going to be able to do that.

Even my successes went wrong. To test our ear for music, twenty sounds were played on a cassette recorder, and the challenge was to indicate which key, from four, the note was played in.

I scored nineteen out of twenty and was chosen to join the school's music group and offered a selection of brass and string instruments, but I declined. I had already joined an afterschool chess class, and had to get through my homework, and eat, before the gruelling boxing training every Tuesday and Thursday evening.

The music test would prove to be the only test I passed at grammar school.

Teachers treated me with a mixture of dismay, and disgust. At the Christmastime exams we put on headphones in a language-lab booth and attempted to translate into English the sentence being spoken by a French voice on an audiotape.

I had absolutely no idea of the answers, and the teacher took me to one side and pleaded with me, almost sympathetically, to make more effort.

When late for the first class of the day, which I often was, some teachers were happy to let me stand outside for the duration of the lesson.

I dreaded going to Geography lessons, where my form master, who was responsible for my welfare at the school, showed consternation at my lack of application.

To fend him off, I adopted a strategy of non-cooperation, which made him even more irate, causing him to froth at the mouth in anger. One exchange went as follows:

'So, Mr. McGale,' he said. 'It's good of you to join us today.'

'Thank you, sir,' I replied carefully, waiting for the imminent attack.

'A fault—that's what I've been thinking of. A fault.'

'What type of fault, sir?' I replied.

'Ah, that's exactly the question I wanted to ask you. What is a fault?'

'It's a fracture in the crust of the planet, sir.'

'And what happens when a fault occurs?'

'What do you mean, sir?'

'I mean what I said, boy. Don't you understand English?'

'Yes, sir,' I said, drawing back as his temper continued to boil.

'"Yes, sir,"' he repeated, exaggeratedly. 'So, when a fault occurs,' he said, leaning in so that I could not avoid the spit coming from his mouth, 'what happens?'

'The parts shift in parallel directions, sir.'

'Parallel directions—that's something you are very familiar

with, but that's not what happens, is it?'

He was now standing so close that he could bite me.

'That's how I understand it, sir.'

'How you understand it, Mr. McGale, is not what we are looking for,' he said, standing upright for effect. 'What we are looking for is a displacement of one side of the fracture with respect to the other, usually in a direction parallel to the fracture. Isn't that right?'

He leaned in again so that I got the message.

'Yes, sir,' I said. 'A displacement of one side of the fracture with respect to the other, usually in a direction parallel to the fracture.'

He strode back to his desk in triumph. The tension in the room lifted.

All around, boys were glad it was me, and not them, who was facing the attack, and I kept my hands firmly on the desk to mask their tremble.

I had already had enough of him and enough of them all.

'Just fucking leave me alone,' I said under my breath. 'You bastard.'

'Which one are you?' said the official voice on the other end of the telephone line.

'Marie, I'm the eldest,' said my seventeen-year-old sister.

'This is the Christian Brothers Grammar School; you'd better come and get your brother.'

'Which one?' Asked my sister.

'Paul, he needs to go home.'

Only weeks had passed since Mum's death, but they'd had enough of Paul and gave him a good-old-fashioned beating to prove it.

But my not-yet fourteen-year-old brother was big and tough, and they had to beat him more than usual to break his will. They wanted tears, an admission that he was a 'disruptive influence', an apology. They got nothing.

Marie went to the school and took him home. He was already taller than her, but she put him into Mum's bed, and they cried together.

His beater was a lay teacher, not a Christian Brother, but at the end of the 1975 school year, shortly after Paul's birthday and little more than three months after Mum's death, a letter arrived addressed to the 'Guardian of Paul McGale.'

It contained a one-page note, on Christian Brothers Grammar School headed notepaper, with his full name written onto the page, Paul Patrick McGale. It was signed by the towering Brother O'Shea and said that my brother's scholarship had been terminated.

At fourteen, it was the beginning of the end for Paul.

CHAPTER SEVEN

Education

My first day at St Patrick's Secondary School, (St Pats), felt like any other bad day at grammar school as Paul and I waited for a meeting with the headmaster, Donal Donnelly.

He was a Gaelic football legend, having been part of the first Tyrone team to win the Ulster Senior Football Championship nearly twenty years before.

It was well known that he was not a man to be messed with.

'Can Christopher McGale come to Mr. Donnelly's office?' a voice had said to the schoolmaster at my first lesson.

On my way there I passed in the foyer a short line of shaven-headed boys standing to attention and spaced as if social distancing. In local jargon they were considered *hard men*, but the skinheads looked decidedly sheepish as they awaited their fate with Mr Donnelly.

Paul was outside the headmaster's office when I arrived.

'Why are we here?' I asked.

'No idea,' he replied.

'Maybe it's to do with Martin,' I offered.

'Maybe,' said Paul.

At fifteen and a half years old, Martin had not joined us on the walk to school that day. He had completed four years at the school, but hardly attended in the months after Mum's death and did not intend to return for his last statutory year in education.

I feared the consequences of my brother's actions and didn't want a repeat of my first day at grammar school, when I had been harangued for being Paul's brother.

Earlier, at school assembly, we had been handed a page with the words of the prayer *Hail Holy Queen* printed on it, which we read aloud with the rest of our new schoolmates at the first assembly of the new school year. It was a prayer that I had recited daily, during my weeklong 'retreat' with the SMA Fathers, at the Newry friary, the summer before.

Mother of Mercy... To thee do we cry, poor banished children of Eve: to thee do we send up our sighs, mourning and weeping in this valley of tears.

I hated that prayer. I wanted to weep in the valley of tears, but I never did.

'Boys, come in here,' said Mr. Donnelly, beckoning us through an open door.

'So, you're Paul and you're Christopher,' he said, as we took seats opposite him.

He was a tall, lean man, but offered none of the threat that we had feared.

'That's right,' we said in unison.

'Sure, I knew your father well—and your mother too. And I know that you've had a terrible time.'

The words made my head drop. I wanted to cry in the valley but recovered quickly as Mr. Donnelly implored us to return to education, believe in ourselves, and live up to our family's good name.

'The McGales were always smart people and I'd hate to see you boys waste your lives,' he said, as Paul nodded.

Since Mum's death six months before, he had been the only person in authority to show any concern.

The next time I had reason to visit Mr. Donnelly's office was to ask permission to go to the hospital to have my right hand X-rayed, having hurt it punching an opponent in a boxing ring.

Soon after that, I threatened a teacher with violence from my brothers unless he stopped picking on me. I had fired a chair at the teacher and ran home before being returned to the school where an understanding Deputy Headmaster promised no further retribution, provided I would accept six anaemic slaps from a leather strap. 'I won't be hard on you,' he vowed.

Later, the thirteen-year-old me sat face-to-face with my form master in a classroom annexe. He was twice my age and responsible for my pastoral care. I had fired the chair I had been sitting on, but in doing so the back separated from the rest and its steel frame shot up into the air, nowhere near my target. We then had a race for the door which I won with the help of an extended foot that he tripped over to whoops of laughter from my classmates.

He was wont to stand behind me and slap me around the back of the head for missing homework or other misdemeanours, and that day in front of my schoolmates called me an unflattering nickname known only to my family.

'I have to be harder on you because the other boys know you're my cousin,' he blustered in the storeroom. I had already taken the leather strap and knew there was nothing more he could do to me. He had recently learned the nickname at the huge funeral of another pillar of the family. Had she not died ten months before, my mother would no doubt have called his, to sort it out.

'If you ever hit me or call me 'tight ass' again I will have my brothers come to your house and sort you out,' I retorted, and left for home once again as he blustered about being threatened.

Fit from boxing in the spring of 1976, I swept the boards at the St Pats sports day, winning medals at 100, 200 and 400 metres, as well as the team relay race.

My points total ensured that my class won the team award for the highest number of points scored, while I won the award for the highest number of points scored by an individual.

The following morning at school assembly in front of four hundred boys, Mr. Donnelly presented me with the George Shannon Perpetual Shield as Sportsman of the Year. The shield was massive—about two and a half feet wide and three and a half feet long—and was adorned with the names of past recipients.

I carried the trophy back to the Headmaster's office, where he promised a photo shoot with a photographer from a local newspaper. Sportsman of the Year or not, that was the last I saw or heard of the trophy.

Mr. Donnelly was losing patience as I had declined to join after-school Gaelic football training. At thirteen, I was required to work at the pub every day between 4pm and 6pm, before handing over to Paul for the evening shift. I then had boxing training on the same days scheduled for Gaelic football practice.

The Headmaster finally gave up on me when I declined to join a group of smarter St Pat's boys in a GCSE initiative that he planned to launch in Year 9.

'Look Chris, this is a great opportunity for you, a chance for you to go to university, to make your parents proud, to graduate.' Graduation was not something I thought about. My only aim in school was to get out as soon as possible.

I was happy to work at the pub as I was paid £3 a week—gambling money.

As a child, when selling raffle tickets at Kate's Bar, it was said that I could sell *snow to the Eskimos* and *sand to the Arabs*.

Back then, I would hang around the pub on a busy Saturday night, enticing regulars to buy raffle tickets for Mum's draw, and soft drinks and crisps for me, until the Salvation Army arrived at 10pm to sell copies of the War Cry, and the sergeant sang *The Old Rugged Cross* from the pub's red and black tiled floor.

It was then time for bed, but not before I swept away the pile of cigarette butts from beneath the feet of men at the bar counter. It was like pushing a brush through snow and it stank.

Now, aged fourteen, I had graduated to marking the scoreboard at the pub, as the adults competed in the Omagh darts league, and learned rapid-fire numeric skills along the way.

The big darts occasion in the years after his death was the *John McGale Memorial* darts competition, and on the night of its annual final the pub would be packed.

Every chalk mark on the blackboard was scrutinised for errors from the gallery behind the players. The moment the last of the player's three tungsten-steel-flighted darts sank into the compressed-hair dartboard his remaining score was chalked up.

In a game of cat and mouse, most of the audience would compute the score, and delight in correcting a score-marker's error, no matter what his age.

A player with a residual score of, say, 131, might chose to shoot for a three-dart finish of treble twenty, treble seventeen, and then double ten. Or he might choose to try treble twenty, treble seven and aim to get out on the bull's-eye.

I was a fully-fledged board-maker at the pub and could price a round of drinks for a darts team in my head, but I would not do maths at school.

What use was school to me? I had a keen interest in world current affairs, fuelled by a diet of television evening news and daily newspapers while working at the pub.

My head, said one teacher, was full of bits of broken glass and bicycle frames. Like many of my schoolmates, I was a 'knucklehead'. But he didn't know me at all. I had already joined adult customers in the Kate's Bar quiz team.

I knew the names of capital cities from around the world: Canberra in Australia, Ottawa in Canada, Bon in West Germany and East Berlin in East Germany. Latin America was a favourite of local quizmasters, so I learned that Bolivia and Paraguay were the only landlocked countries in South America, that Lima was the capital of Peru and Montevideo of Uruguay, and that the latter country was the first to win the World Cup when host in 1930.

I knew that pi was '3.142' but had no concept of the equation *pi r squared*; and that the Dow Jones and the FT Ordinary Share indexes were made up of 30 shares, but knew little about their constituents and nothing about how an index is calculated.

Earlier that year, in January 1976, while rambling with friends by the fairy tree in Cunningham's Field near St Pat's, a message was shouted from boy to boy; 'The McGales are wanted at home. Their granny is dead.'

I had just passed my thirteenth birthday and had not seen her since Mum's funeral ten months before, as the weekly visits to the hills above Drumquin had become a thing of the past.

Birthday celebrations had also become history. The birthday cards that the SMA Fathers had sent, ever since I could remember, died with Mum's subscription.

With Granny's death, we no longer had a blood parent or grandparent alive in the world.

Omagh Boxing Club, front row second left,
with trainer Paddy Crawford and
Fr Michael Doherty - circa 1977

CHAPTER EIGHT

The Gambler

At fifteen, I sat theatre-style with two hundred boys and girls on the floor of the Omagh Boys & Girls Club clubhouse, as the winners of the 1978 annual awards were announced, and no-one was more surprised than me when I won the trophy for Best Competitor of the Year.

While the Clubman of the Year, Clubwoman of the Year, Best Sportsman, and Best Sportswoman prizes went to deserving 'team players', my participation at the club involved competing on my own against opponents in the boxing ring, with the adult club leaders at chess, and at 8-ball pool with anyone who would play.

Having spent years perfecting my pool skills on the Kate's Bar baize, I was generating a regular source of income, hustling all-comers at the pub in ever-bigger cash games.

My usual chess partner was a St Pat's schoolteacher who, a year before, had taught me a valuable lesson about gambling. A modest-stakes horseracing man himself, he was the club leader on a weekend-away in Donegal and watched as a low-stakes game of fun-poker escalated.

Pence turned into pounds as a boy three years my senior raised the stakes. I was losing and my concerned mentor intervened to stop the game.

It was late and I was already several pounds in deficit, but

I was not happy to stop.

'Let's get out the chess board instead,' said the club-leader, as I continued to hold the playing cards that I had brought with me on the trip.

'Nah, that's boring,' I replied, hoping to get a chance to restart the game.

'Have a titter of wit and give me those cards,' he demanded, his patience exhausted, 'and everyone sit down here. I want to show you something.'

We watched as he passed every one of the fifty-two playing cards from one hand to the other, focusing on the face of each. He repeated the process, then placed the pack of cards face down on the table and peeled one card after another from the top of the deck.

'The four of clubs, the queen of hearts, the eight of diamonds, the king of spades,' he said, calling out the name of each card before turning it face up, until all fifty-two had been correctly identified.

'Jesus, that's amazing,' I said.

It was a parable for me. There is always a better player at the table. It was time to go to bed.

I was generally cash-rich, as I was being paid to work at the pub, could rely on a steady stream of income from hustling customers on the pool table, was the pub's bookie's runner, and had become better at winning regularly on horse racing.

Before my 4pm Saturday work shift behind the bar counter, my job at the betting shop saw me running back and forth to the bookie's, about 50 metres away, carrying bets for the pub customers. Woe-betide me if I failed to place the bet on time.

I would take two giant leaps down the wooden, six-tread, stairwell and dash out the side door, being careful not to clatter into a passer-by as I leapt onto the footpath. From there I would adopt the pose of Roy Rogers on horseback, whipping my hip with a sweep of my right hand, urging

Trigger to go faster.

The shop was owned by the legendary gambler, Barney Curley, who hailed from nearby Irvinestown. The only day I didn't work as a runner was when Barney was in town, which was rare.

A few years before, despite being teetotal, he had launched The Cheltenham Arms, a huge Omagh pub. It had been funded by gambling winnings but did not prove to be a good investment.

I was thrilled by tales of Barney's successes and sought to adopt his betting principles; core among which was that patience is required to win when betting on racehorses.

In practice, that meant studying the form for hours and selecting one or two races from the dozens listed on a busy Saturday. That allowed for bigger stakes and bigger winnings.

I first knew I wanted to be legendary, like Barney, three months after Mum's death in June 1975, when Barney, a former Jesuit seminarian who left after four years having contracted tuberculosis, pulled-off the biggest betting coup in the history of British or Irish gambling.

In betting shops around Ireland, he bet £15,000 on his own horse, Yellow Sam, through dozens of 'off-track' associates. Despite the late rush of money for a horse previously considered slow, Yellow Sam's winning odds were 20/1—meaning Barney won £300,000 (worth about £2.5m today).

In the days before mobile phones, Bellewstown Racecourse, a small track north of Dublin, had only two phone lines, one for the racecourse officials, from which the Extel news agency could report the on-track Starting Price (SP) to the high-street bookie shops, and another in a public phone box.

As Barney's good luck would have it, the Bellewstown Extel line became defective early that day and a friend of his spent nearly half an hour before the race began occupying the public phone booth, apparently talking with a dying aunt.

Had the 'off-track' betting surge been reported to the 'on-track' bookies, Yellow Sam's starting price would have been dramatically lower than 20/1.

A slow horse got a whole lot faster, but nothing illegal had transpired and the bookies were obliged to pay. They were so incensed they conspired to pay his winnings in single one-pound notes—a mound that filled more than one hundred bags.

Studying form was something that came easy to me. The past performance figures for every horse in a race are listed vertically in narrow newsprint columns, in a way that resembles marriage and death notices. I could 'see' the data contained within the form guide, long after I had read it. I could see a picture of the typographical text exactly as I had viewed it in the first place and could later recall a horse's precise form details from the racing newssheet that I had read earlier that day.

'A photographic memory, just like Barney Curley,' said one old mentor.

Aged sixteen, I saw out my last statutory school year, studying for a City & Guilds Craft Certificate at Omagh Tech. In the evenings I was one of the youngest attendees at the Drop-In Centre, a place sponsored by the Western Education & Library Board and staffed by social workers.

Despite the good intentions, it was not long before it acquired the nickname, *The Drop-Out Centre*. I used the facility to hone two skills: eight ball pool and poker.

Money won on the pool table on a busy Friday at Kate's would be recycled into increased stakes on Saturday afternoon's horse racing and any winnings still intact the following day would be made ready for the big Sunday night poker game at the Drop-in Centre.

It was dealer's choice, and we played Texas Holdem, Five

Card Draw poker, Seven Card Stud poker and Southern Cross.

Always wanting to keep the game moving, I gathered the cards between hands and passed them to the new dealer, and soon acquired a nickname, The Dealer, or in the vernacular, *The Daler*.

I never relaxed during a game, and to the annoyance of other players, pushed those around me to get on, play their hand, 'shit or get off the pot'.

Although I was the youngest player, I was considered the most fearless. The controlled aggression necessary for success in a boxing ring was also crucial in poker.

Arriving at the Sunday game with a good pot of money available to lose, was also important. That offered me a bigger club with which to batter my opponents, helping me force them into financial submission.

My behaviour didn't make me popular, but I had already decided that winning was more important than being liked.

I regularly sought to raise the betting stakes early in a game, and any player, or players, willing to match those stakes could be expected to have a good hand of cards. Otherwise, they could expect that that game might be their last of the night. In facing me down, they knew that they would either win big or lose their lot.

Given the sums that I was gambling every week, I learned to stay quiet about my winnings and losings. To keep schtum.

That way, the only person affected was me.

I had begun to realise that I was a good loser. Hard work had made me disciplined at horses, pool, and poker, and any loss was always tempered by an expectation of winning next time.

What I didn't realise was that my greatest strength in the gambling world – a lack of fear – was also my greatest weakness. No individual bet was enough. I wanted to keep grinding up the ante—and win big.

In Mum's bedroom with Best Competitor trophy and holy statues – aged fifteen

CHAPTER NINE

Good Friday

'Oh no, not another McGale with rotten teeth,' said my NHS dentist as I approached his chair. It was a perverse attempt to encourage dental hygiene. I was used to that dentist saying horrible things about our teeth; but didn't need the advice.

'My recommendation is that we take out all your teeth and mould a full set of dentures once the gums settle down,' said another dental surgeon a few months later.

'In any event, you will be in hospital for some time and this way we can fix your teeth once and for all. We can do it under general anaesthetic, so you won't feel a thing.'

It was April 1979, and I was sitting beside my hospital bed at a Belfast sanatorium, listening intently as the surgeon spoke to my seventeen-year-old brother on the other side of a cubicle curtain.

There was hardly a day in the four years that had passed since Mum's death, that Paul had not consumed large amounts of alcohol.

He clandestinely stored vodka in a soda water bottle on a bedside table, in a ruse given away by the strong smell from his breath of undiluted alcohol, and suffered a seizure on our first night at the hospital.

He was given intravenous Paraldehyde at bedtime for a week to help him with the effects of alcohol withdrawal syndrome.

I advised the doctors of the prescription, as an on-call doctor had recently injected the brown-coloured medicine into his hip when he had fitted in the bed beside me.

A side effect of his earlier attempts to cut back on the booze was Delirium Tremens (DTs), like when he woke me in the middle of the night to summon my help to apprehend his drinking buddies, who were raiding the downstairs spirits store.

I stood barefoot in my underwear 'standing guard,' while he unlocked the storeroom and raced inside to chase out the thieves. There were no thieves.

Just one week before our arrival at hospital, four years after my fight debut, I had fought what was to be my last boxing match.

I was already, for the second time, a Tyrone Juvenile Champion, and had progressed to the Mid-Ulster finals for the first time. I had not proceeded to the Mid-Ulsters when I won my first title, due to Mum's death.

In all, I had contested the final of four out of the last five Tyrone Championships and took a one-year sabbatical on the other occasion.

I had never had more confidence. I expected to win, to become Mid-Ulster Champion, to progress to the Ulster Finals at Belfast's Ulster Hall and join a rarefied list of local boxing heroes who had won Ulster titles for the good name of Omagh.

I had begun to dream of being the Ulster Champion and maybe one day box for Ireland.

'This guy spars with McGuigan,' said the coach from another club to mine, as I climbed into the ring. He was referring to Barry McGuigan, the Commonwealth Games Gold Medallist. The words didn't affect me, as I focused on the bandages wrapped tightly around my hands to support my wrists and reinforce the impact of my punches.

I took my place in the ring, with the sparring partner of a boxer who would later become the WBA World Featherweight

Champion, and got hammered.

Everything went in slow motion. He picked me off in defence and attack and, after one barrage of punches during the second round, the referee stopped the fight to escort me back to the red corner.

Blood streamed from my nose onto my yellow Omagh Boxing Club vest.

The fight was over.

It was a lonely ride home on the team bus as I dealt with the embarrassment of my defeat, the ignominy. To lose was painful, but to be hammered was unbearable. I didn't think it was possible.

I knew I had fast hands. I could hit hard. I could jab and move. I had never been fitter or stronger. I had trained myself to believe that I could beat anybody.

In the darkness of the minibus, I gingerly felt the bruises around my head and picked delicately the hardened blood from my nose until I could breathe through it again.

In the silence I looked around to find that the heads of all my colleagues were turned towards the windows. Most of them had been in my shoes before.

There was no one there to meet me when I arrived back at John Street that evening. Everyone had their own fight with the world and no sibling ever saw me box.

I made my way to the bathroom at the top of the stairs and stared in the mirror. My nose was swollen, and black rings had begun to appear under my eyes. My right ear was red and raw and extremely sore to touch. I cleared my nose and spat the iron-tasting blood from my mouth and washed it down the sink.

'Maybe I should have showered,' I thought as I lay on my back in bed and smelled the sweaty stink of my body.

But my head had been too sore to contemplate washing all around it and the immersion heater would take too long.

Besides, the bathroom was too cold to strip bare.

Instead I cuddled up under the blankets and drifted off to sleep to the steady rhythm of the pub's ice-making machine that stood on a shelf above my head, from which I had earlier placed cubes in a facecloth to make an icepack for my nose and eyes. Its location above me was a legacy of when the bedroom was a darts room for the pub.

'What happened to you?' said a sympathetic doctor two days later when I visited the surgery on a busy Monday morning. He was a friend of Dad's who had always offered advice and support in the thirteen years since his death.

'Boxing, Doctor,' I said. 'It keeps me fit, Doctor,' I continued quickly, seeking to avoid a repetition of Mum's, 'Boxing, weren't you better reared than that?'

'Your nose is clearly broken,' he said, confirming what I knew. 'There is no point having it X-rayed today. Instead, I will make an appointment for you with an ENT Consultant who will repair it.'

'Repair it how?'

'Break it again, and re-set it,' he said dryly, 'and realign the septum, which appears to be affecting your breathing.'

At sixteen, it was time to retire from the boxing ring, but within days I had learned that it hadn't only been fear of my opponent that had led to my lethargic performance.

On the morning of April 13th, 1979, Good Friday, Paul and I went for X-rays at the Tyrone County Hospital. The X-rays showed that he had a shadow on both lungs and that I had a penny-sized cavity in my right lung. We had gone for the hospital checks after Martin had been diagnosed with pleurisy and had fluid drained from his chest.

All three of us were diagnosed with tuberculosis, a once-fatal bacterial disease, also known as consumption, mostly associated with filthy living conditions and the urban poor.

Martin was lucky, since the drain largely removed the disease, while Paul and I faced a period of hospitalisation. We were sent home to pack our bags and directed to make our way to the Forster Green Hospital, Belfast, for a long internment.

Paul suffered from the common TB symptoms; a persistent cough and phlegm on the lungs. He would regularly wake from the bed that we shared in John Street, and, with a cough and a roar, would speed the TB-contaminated green slime from his throat onto a paper tissue or the bedroom carpet between our bed and Martin's.

Prior to going to Forster Green, I did not have any of Paul's symptoms, nor was I aware of the other tell-tale signs—weight loss and night sweats.

We arrived at the hospital around seven pm on Good Friday, were examined by the duty doctor and were given bed baths. I became aware of the stink and sweatiness of my skin, which the attendant nurse explained was a sure sign of TB in my system.

It was Holy Saturday when I stripped bare-chested and was X-rayed once again. The initial prognosis was confirmed. The consultant indicated that the infection was confined to the cavity and with effective treatment I would be out of there quickly.

The treatment plan for Paul made him swear; it required him to stay for up to twelve weeks, taking him through his eighteenth birthday on June 17, 1979.

We were prescribed a combined therapy of antibiotics called Isoniazid, and Rifampicin, a bullet-shaped tablet that turned our urine rusty red. That drug is also used to treat leprosy.

After a few days, I got the news that my stay in hospital would now be months not weeks.

Rifampicin was having an adverse effect on my liver and I would have to revert to an antibiotic called Streptomycin—a drug that required intramuscular delivery via a large syringe.

An invisible X was drawn from top to bottom on my

backside, after which a finger was pressed at the intersection of the two lines. Into this spot on my hip a needle was plunged and discharged for about ten seconds.

The needle required a trained eye, as a badly guided sharp could hit the sciatic nerve and paralyse me.

The twice daily jabs made it painful to sit. When watching television, I would hunch over the back of a reading chair, stretching the pain out of the muscles in my hip.

It was important not to tense the muscle when receiving the needle, as it would lock around the syringe leaving it bruised and sore. When on one occasion I allowed a nurse to try the needle through the front of my thigh, it caused a bruise so bad I hobbled around on one leg for a week.

Paul and I did nothing together. After years of fighting our respective battles, we had nothing in common.

All the family had had the BCG vaccination at school, and I blamed Paul's boozing for my being in hospital.

Yet at the hospital, he was *as sober as a judge* and spent most of his waking hours in a chair beside his bed, wading through crosswords, and books supplied by the hospital library, but hardly said a word.

Reading books was alien to me, but I read newspapers cover to cover, hoovering data and information for no-one's benefit but my own.

I wandered around the extensive hospital grounds and filled the daily monotony by playing draughts with the older inmates, whom I could never beat. I made stuffed, furry elephants from sewing materials provided by the hospital's occupational therapy team—cuddly toys that I hoped to sell for cash to future visitors.

Televised horseracing from the 2000 Guineas meeting at Newmarket, the Epsom Derby, and the summer festivals at Royal Ascot, York, and Glorious Goodwood, eased the boredom of hospital life.

I placed bets back in Omagh via the mobile hospital payphone and took low-stake wagers from the old residents in adjacent wards. At sixteen it was my debut at being a bookie.

At Kate's Bar, I liked to chat with old customers and enjoyed their tales of yore. At Forster Green I became the regular walking partner of an old patient, Mr Harrison, a worldly chap who spent his early life in the merchant navy.

'I'm going to travel the world too,' I said. 'I want to go to New York to see Madison Square Garden and I have cousins in Philadelphia,' one of whom had travelled with her husband to Omagh a year before for Noelle's wedding.

'You won't be able to go to America son.'

'Why not?'

'Because you have TB, they won't let you into America with TB on your record.'

'Damn, I never thought of that.'

On another day during one of our circuits around the hospital grounds, I said in a throwaway remark, 'one day, when we get out of here, I'll come to see you in Belfast.'

The pensioner's swift reply took the sixteen-year-old me aback; 'Ah no son, we're not the same....' He never finished the sentence. The missing word was, *religion.*

Paul and I sat side by side for months and spoke only when necessary.

Being an hour from home, our only regular visitor was our Belfast pharmacist uncle Mick, who came by every Thursday evening with a copy of the Belfast Telegraph.

A man of few words, he made his way through the newspaper, pointed out articles of interest, and, reflecting his precise nature, always left behind a crisp £5 note for our needs.

'What are your plans?' he always said to me as I walked him off the premises. I knew he was asking about my return to education.

I had seen out my final school year at Omagh Tech, and had completed the exam for my City & Guilds craft certificate in Carpentry and Joinery, while supervised by a teacher in an empty hospital ward, but had no plan to continue in education.

'Education's easy carried,' he would repeat, as Mum had, in Grandad's Drumquin vernacular.

His plan was to visit a hotel for a nightcap and a cigar on his way back across The city, a thought that always drew a wicked smile when I wished him well for his evening at the Wellington Park Hotel.

Like most Belfast hostelries a decade after the start of the war, entry was blocked by wire mesh and a security gate, as indiscriminate sectarianism remained a threat to everyone, even a gentleman like Michael, as he was popularly known outside the family.

Many years later he sold the North Belfast pharmacy he had founded forty years before and moved to Spain, after being pistol-whipped and ordered to leave the largely protestant area by a hooded assailant whom he recognised.

'I think your mother sent me on that journey,' said a family friend years later, telling me of another sectarian assault.

He was a former Kate's Bar barrel-boy, who with his teenage brother had worked with Mum for many years. Three times a week, they washed and refilled hundreds of bottles from giant barrels supplied by Arthur Guinness & Co, attached *Bottled by John McGale* labels, and plunged corks via a machine that took a finger off one of my elder cousins.

The brothers were part of my formative years, but even more so for Martin and Paul. Mum was very fond of them both.

On that night, he was driving through Omagh's empty streets to collect his sister from a friend's house. 'It was nearly two am when I came down Church Hill and saw that the road was blocked by a blue Ford Escort car, which had stopped at the junction with John Street, opposite the pub. All four doors were open, so I got out of my car to see what was going on.

'I saw four twenty-something men kicking at someone's head. It was Paul. They stopped when they saw me. They ran right past me and drove off down the Kevlin Road. I didn't recognise any of them.

Paul was choking on the blood. I had received first-aid training through work, so I opened his airways and put him in the recovery position. A neighbour brought a blanket and called an ambulance,' he said.

When I saw Paul the following day, his head was swollen to the size of a medicine ball, his face and neck were purple and bruised, his mouth was bloodied and swollen, and his arms and torso were bandaged and cut.

He had spent the hours before at a neighbouring pub, after working the evening shift at ours. It was the summer of 1978. He had just turned seventeen.

On June 30, 1979, nearly two weeks after Paul's eighteenth birthday, I was excited after watching highlights of a brutal fight for the WBC World Welterweight Championship on Saturday afternoon sports television; when 'Hands of Stone' Roberto Duran dethroned Carlos Palomino at Madison Square Garden.

By now, I knew that TB had played a big part in my final fight flop, and my dream of fighting for Ireland. Paul was to blame for my being incarcerated instead of fighting in the Ulster Hall.

The fight excitement soon turned to anger. I could have been the Ulster Champion by now if it wasn't for him.

Gone was my chance of ever fighting against America's

Golden Gloves amateur champions who regularly toured Ireland, and with TB on my record, he had killed my chance of ever living in America.

'Cheers,' was the only thing he said, when someone brought him a meal or changed his bedsheets at Forster Green. That maddened me too.

I was scundered. It was all down to him and the bloody booze.

I wanted confrontation but nothing I could say riled him. He simply ignored me.

Unlike him, I never suffered growing pains, and even though I thought he would probably beat me now that he was sober, I wanted to annoy him, to make him fight me, but he just looked back blankly, disdainful. The knowledge that he was still superior was hard to take.

And so, unprovoked, I attacked him verbally as he sat with a book on his lap. I listed a charge-sheet of offences against me and the whole family including knocking to the ground the cooked Christmas Day turkey that had shattered to smithereens on the tiled hallway floor below.

His calm reply stunned me. 'I'm sorry, but I don't remember any of that,' he said, and turned back to his book.

Paul was discharged soon after.

From then on, I was like a prisoner preparing to go before the Governor when my consultant conducted his Friday rounds, until I was finally released from Forster Green Hospital on Friday, September 21, 1979.

I had arrived there on Good Friday nearly six months before.

Later I wondered whether, even though he had just turned eighteen, Paul was already suffering from brain damage caused by years of alcohol abuse and the beating he had taken a year before. The four months he spent in hospital proved to be no more than a respite from the multi-year battle he had with booze.

Many years before, Dad had worked at Holy Joe's, an East Belfast pub not far from Forster Green, where he served drinks to the largely-Protestant, and shipyard worker clientele. The pub was so-called because the owner refused to serve the working men at the end of a shift until they had first gone home and handed over their wages to their wives. With Mum, they fostered a non-political, cross-community, pub culture in Omagh, which did not survive much after the start of The Troubles.

The two Ulster Tribes, Catholic and Protestant, had been in conflict since the Plantation of Ulster four hundred years before, and as the violence of The Troubles erupted all around in 1969, people reverted to their own tribe whether they liked it or not.

Ten years after that, during the summer of our incarceration, a thirty-three-year-old father of three, and former pub-regular, was shot dead near his home after leaving a sweetshop at the entrance of the Christian Brother's Grammar School.

A Protestant, he had grown up in our Gallows Hill neighbourhood, but stopped coming to the pub some years before, having become a part-time soldier in the Ulster Defence Regiment (UDR).

That morning he was on his way to work as a gravedigger. He was shot by the passenger of a preying car after he crossed the road. Bullet holes in a wall behind a street bench remained unrepaired months later. It seemed that no-one could summon the courage to go there.

His IRA killer, who would later receive two life sentences, knew him well and I knew them both.

My last memory of John 'Whitey' Hannigan, a happy, handsome, man with a shock of fair hair, was at Mum's graveside, watching streams of tears flood down his face as he stood, spade in hand, beside her open grave.

Back in John Street, our bedroom now contained three new single beds, and the ice-making machine had been relocated to the kitchen below. The spit-filled carpet had been replaced, and the freshly painted room left no trace of the mess it had been before.

It no longer presented any threat of contamination; it had been fumigated.

CHAPTER TEN

Alive & Dangerous

Northern Ireland was a dangerous place to grow up. Before my tenth birthday in 1972, I was nearby when a bomb exploded at Woolworths. The store was in temporary accommodation in George's Street near the Sacred Heart Church, its town centre shop having already been bombed. I was in front of the Court House, on a deserted High Street, less than one hundred metres away, and felt the ground tremble beneath me and air pull me towards the narrow street, but I was not hurt.

Six years later a car bomb blast sucked the windows out of Strule River-facing Omagh Tech classroom from which we had been evacuated. It devastated a pub and several shops on nearby Bridge Street.

As I entered the school premises that morning, I saw the caretaker hoist the Union Jack on the forecourt.

'What's the occasion?' I asked.

'Prince Charles' birthday,' came the reply. It was November 1978.

For several years prior to that, the constant use of car bombs to destroy the commercial centres of Omagh and other Ulster towns and cities, meant that vehicular access was restricted by a Control Zone. A single-entry checkpoint was manned by armed police and soldiers in Market Street at the bottom of the town, and all the other roads were permanently blocked by huge reinforced concrete bollards or levered steel gates through which vehicles could exit in the daytime.

At the top of the town, an exit-only barrier stood on the corner of John Street opposite our pub – which was outside the permanent barricade.

When the gates were closed, the streets were manned intermittently by army foot patrols, while armed police, the Royal Ulster Constabulary (RUC), in unmarked cars circled the surrounding roads; such that the centre became a place that most people chose to avoid after dark.

Among those brave enough to venture into the militarised zone were old men who refused to give up the habit of a lifetime – an evening pint – such as those who visited pubs like uncle Brian's, Bear's Paw, a town centre venue named after another in Liverpool.

A gentle soul, Brian, who succumbed to a heart attack a few years later, had moved back to Omagh from Glasgow with his wife Sally and three of what would be their four boys. Initially they lived above our pub with our then-bachelor father, before Brian bought his own pub.

Sally was the aunt of Strabane's Paul Brady, a member of Ireland's folk super-group Planxty, who sometimes jammed unannounced with Omagh's guitar virtuoso, Arty McGlynn, at the Bear's Paw, and the mere prospect of their appearance there ensured a steady flow of evening-time customers in an otherwise deserted town centre.

Now fourteen, I was still young enough not to fear the might of the military forces or the prospect of a sectarian beating, and I never considered that I might go to jail or get shot dead while roaming the streets of Omagh.

One evening in early 1977, I came across two older boys whom I knew, who were painting abusive graffiti about the Queen's forthcoming Silver Jubilee visit to Belfast on the blank canvas wall that used to be the facade to the bombed Town Hall.

'What the fuck are you doing here?' shouted the taller of the boys.

'Nothing,' I spluttered, 'I'm on my way to Uncle Brian's.'

'Let's get out of here,' said the other. I ran back towards Kate's Bar with them, until we stopped running at John Street Corner and looked down Kevlin Road.

'Not a word now Chris, not a fucking word,' said the tall boy in hushed tones when we saw on the road ahead darting soldiers on foot patrol. 'Just keep walking.'

I did, until we crossed paths with the SLR-carrying troops.

'Evening lads,' said a friendly squaddie at the front of the six-man group spread out on either side of Kevlin Road. They were among the forty thousand troops and armed police aiming to bring peace to the streets of Northern Ireland: one armed member of the security forces for every forty of the population. In all three-hundred-thousand British soldiers served there during the conflict.

'Evening sir,' we said together.

Being teenagers, we were not expected to carry ID, but I knew that my companions were concerned that the canisters of spray paint in their jacket pockets would be found.

'We're just going home sir, from the youth club sir, to there,' said the tall boy, pointing to the row of houses at the top of the old cow commons, on Gallows Hill, behind our pub.

'Okay lads, off you go on your way,' said the cheery patrol leader on that mild winter's night, without taking our names and addresses.

The following morning the graffiti had been painted over and the Queen and the citizens of Omagh were none the wiser.

Even though I had done nothing wrong, I was relieved to see the freshly painted walls of the Town Hall.

The Troubles meant that trouble was never far away.

Not long afterwards, following a three-round brawl, I lost

the second of my four Tyrone County Juvenile Boxing Championships finals.

I need not have feared that I would have to fight again my not-yet-fifteen-year-old, Strabane opponent. He would soon become the youngest republican prisoner in the eight-years of The Troubles so far.

A relaxation of the Control Zone laws allowed Sunday morning and evening church-goers to drive up to the top of the town, past the Town Hall, and park on the roads in front of the Courthouse on their way to the Sacred Heart, Catholic, church, and St Columba's, Church of Ireland, church.

It was six months after the graffiti incident, on a bright summer's evening, that I pulled on a Halloween facemask that I found on our living room sofa.

The clown's mask entirely covered my head, and I headed off with another boy to play 'car-tag' with the oncoming Sunday-evening worship traffic, until we heard the screech of brakes from a car on its way back down the hill from the Courthouse.

When the car did a U-turn in the street below, we guessed correctly that it was an unmarked police car and ran for home.

I pulled off the hot facemask and legged it into John Street. We then cut into a side street known as 'Bobby's Entry' and ran past a five-foot square concrete roadblock that had been placed there by the Army.

As the police car ground to a halt at the bottom of the entry, we raced on. Our attention-seeking act had attracted the wrong attention.

'Stop or I'll shoot!' said the policeman, twenty metres behind us, but we ran on and at the end of the entry faced two machine-gun-wielding RUC officers who were running up Church Hill towards us. They had abandoned their car at the steel barrier on John Street Corner below.

We stopped, exhausted, at the back of St Columba's Church.

'What's going on?' I demanded to know.

We had reached home territory and could see the pub down the hill. The overweight policeman who had shouted 'stop or I'll shoot' emerged from the entry, gasping for breath after his 100-metre uphill run.

There was a large R on the arm of his uniform, indicating that he was a member of the RUC Reserve force. I knew him, as he ran a local business, but guessed that he didn't know me. The R added to the enmity as many of the RUC reservists had previously been members of the B-Specials, a fifty-year-old militia force that was mobilised in August 1969 and disbanded just eight months later. Half my life before, when I was six or seven, my siblings and I had watched from upstairs windows as the B-Specials brutalised civil rights protesters on John Street Corner below.

'You could have been shot, why didn't you stop?' he spluttered.

But I had no fear of the fat bastard with the machine gun, whose belly preceded him up the hill.

'I'm one of the McGales, of John Street, and we have done nothing wrong,' I blasted.

'You may not have done anything wrong today,' growled our bearded pursuer, 'but you nearly caused a riot with that mask last night.'

I didn't know it then, but Paul, then sixteen, had been drunk at a neighbouring John Street pub and had gone outside to remonstrate with the marching Orangemen as they passed. When the police had made it onto the premises, neither Paul nor the mask could be found.

'Look,' I said, 'it wasn't me. I don't drink, and I wasn't in any pub.'

And with that, my companion and I marched off.

If that was a minor foray with death, I pushed the limits

a year later when I accepted an offer to ride a motorbike without having any idea of how to do so.

Keen to impress, a relative stranger offered the gathered group of Gallows Hill boys a chance to ride his brand-new Suzuki 250cc motorbike. I watched an experienced older boy steer the awesome machine a hundred metres up and down past a straight row of cottages, and as the instructions sounded elementary, I volunteered to go next.

'Push the button to turn it on, put the bike into gear with your left foot, turn the accelerator with your right hand, let the clutch out slowly with your left hand and the bike will move off.'

It was clear enough to me as I pulled on his helmet and got on board the motorbike. With the press of a button the engine buzzed below, but when I pulled the accelerator back too far and released the clutch too quickly, the bike reared-up onto its back wheel and sped off down the road with me clinging on for dear life.

I clung on to the handlebar with the accelerator fully extended, the bike still in first gear and the engine screaming as the machine careered down the road, with me performing an unplanned, exhibition-style wheelie.

After a ten-second eternity, I let go of the handlebars, slid from a vertical position, landed on my backside and scraped along the road, tearing the bottom out of my trousers.

Ahead, I watched as the bike bounced from side to side and narrowly missed cars parked on the right-hand side of the street, before settling with its accelerator jammed against the road, screeching and firing flames from an exhaust pipe.

Sitting on the road, I turned to see the owner and my buddies frozen on the kerbside behind me, and cried for somebody to do something before the bike exploded.

My stomach churned and my limbs jellied, as I experienced real shock for the first time in my life. I was lucky to escape with no more than bruising to my backside and to my pride.

Twice as a child I was hit by a car while playing 'chicken' on John Street, and once as an adolescent I was hit darting out from behind a delivery truck on my way to pick up the racing pages for a day scheming school.

Once, in a drink-drive incident, I was jammed in the back seat with three members of the Kate's Bar quiz team when a car banked onto its two offside wheels as the driver attempted to right himself after driving too fast into a sharp bend.

Another time, I spun my brother-in-law's car on the M1 Motorway, having lost control attempting to pass a drinks can over my shoulder at seventy-miles-per-hour.

The front driver's-side tyre was shredded as I braked hard and the car turned on a sixpence.

A partially open window caused a vacuum inside the vehicle, sucking a cloud of grit and grime from the road below that stuck to my hair, face, and arms.

Later, while driving in Belfast, I reached to adjust the radio and crashed into the back of a stationary vehicle that had braked to a standstill to avoid a dog that had crossed in front of it.

We crashed on Northumberland Street, a no-mans-land link-road between the Falls Road and Shankill Road.

I was set to be fined for careless driving but was delighted when the police arrived at the scene from the nearby Tennent Street RUC station. I did not wish to become another sectarian victim, another statistic, among the three-thousand-five-hundred deaths of The Troubles, nor the near-fifty thousand who were injured.

It was my seventh road-related incident.

If I was happy to see armed security forces as protectors in the Belfast no-man's land, that was not the case in Omagh, in late 1980, around the time of my eighteenth birthday.

Tribal tensions were high as the IRA and INLA had just ended a 53-day hunger strike and it was the early hours of the morning when we left a local nightclub to find the only exit route blocked by UDR armoured vehicles.

I wasn't keen to see if they were friend or foe, especially when empty Coke, Lucozade, and other glass bottles that had been stored neatly at the rear of the premises, began to rain upon the military.

Earlier that year I had attended a fabulous concert by Irish supergroup Thin Lizzy, at the nearby Enniskillen, Forum Leisure Centre. No major acts toured Northern Ireland then, a legacy of The Troubles and the Miami Showband massacre five years before. Then a botched Ulster Volunteer Force (UVF) attempt to plant a bomb in the Dublin band's minibus killed two of the perpetrators and the remaining gang shot dead three and wounded the other two fleeing band members. The killings were carried out at a bogus security forces checkpoint, by the Glenanne Gang that included serving members of the RUC and UDR. Numbering as many as twenty-five in all, they were responsible for the murders of one-hundred-and-twenty mostly-civilian Catholics between 1972 and 1980; including eighty deaths in the 'murder triangle' area of Armagh and East Tyrone, and the 1974 car bomb slaughters on the streets of Dublin and Monaghan.

The gig, part of Lizzy's *Live and Dangerous* world tour, when the band played tracks from what has often been described as the greatest live album ever made, had been transferred from Bundoran, Co. Donegal, after the local Canon objected to the event being held there on Maundy Thursday.

My pride and joy was a Thin Lizzy sweatshirt acquired that evening that I wore continuously for the rest of the year.

With the glass bottle ammunition fast running out, a few of us sought to circumvent the riot by making our way across a field at the rear of the venue towards an adjacent residential estate. The field turned out to be a bog that we struggled to navigate in the darkness, but that didn't matter as we approached a hedgerow intending to make our way to a nearby house.

'Don't fucking move,' roared a local accent, before I was dragged through the ditch, thrown onto my back, and lay staring up the barrel of a UDR-man's SLR.

'I've done nothing wrong,' I protested, before being bundled into the back of an army jeep.

Along with a friend I sat in the vehicle for hours outside Omagh RUC station before we were sent on our way before dawn. It was the third time in my life that I had got too close to an SLR, but there was no harm done, other than the neck being torn out of my Live and Dangerous sweatshirt.

Control Zone barrier on John Street Corner
– mid-1970s

CHAPTER ELEVEN

Back to School

On one wet Saturday morning at the end of March 1980, the only 'academic' thing on my mind was analysing the racing columns of the Sporting Life newspaper where I scanned and consumed the form figures of the 30 horses that would later contest the annual Grand National horserace. With rain pouring down on Aintree Racecourse, I was looking for 'value'.

'The horse doesn't know what price it is,' I recalled an old sage say, and, conscious that lots of good horses had been withdrawn due to the heavy underfoot conditions, alighted on the mud-loving Ben Nevis—an unfancied 40/1 shot that had fallen in the 30-fence race a year before.

Grand National Day at our pub came a close second to being at Aintree Racecourse itself.

A collective roar went up at Kate's Bar when the race-starter's tape was raised for the mud-fest. Anxious faces rose and fell throughout the four-and-a-half-miles of the race, just like the four-legged warriors on which their money rode.

Over the course of the marathon race, the runners and riders attempted to leap over the eight-foot-high Chair fence, twice negotiate the big fall on the landing side of the Becher's Brook ditch and muster one last effort as they pushed towards the Canal Turn for the second and final time.

When Ben Nevis scaled the peaks of Aintree's birch fences

and at last crossed the finish line, he was first of the four leg-weary survivors, out of thirty that started. I had won £125.

Wanting to win big, I put £100 on West Germany to win the UEFA EURO 1980 football championship that was still three months away. When Horst Hrubesch headed a last-minute goal in the June final, my £100 had turned into £300 and I loaned it all to a rock band that I managed, Casper, headed by a former schoolmate who had followed a similar course to me, all the way from the Christian Brothers primary and grammar schools to Omagh Tech.

With new Marshall amps now in place, Casper could get on with touring the country.

The band leader called me 'the moneyman' and I was, as one pub wag observed, 'The youngest impresario in Ireland!'

For a few years I had been organising gigs at which Casper played support to leading Irish performers such as *Mamas Boys*, Rob Strong, whose son Andrew would later star in *The Commitments,* and Gerry Anderson's *Toejam*, where the super-cool, latter-day radio and television broadcaster, liked to refer to himself as Gerry/Londongerry.

Londongerry was a funny word for me, and Londonderry even more so. I heard it daily on the television and radio news, as its people bore the brunt of The Troubles, but no-one ever said Londonderry to me and meant it.

I was eighteen years old before an Omagh Tech schoolmate told me he was planning to go to the Londonderry College of Technology. 'Derry Tech?' I replied, incredulous.

No longer part of the family business, with a buddy from a neighbouring pub, I spent that summer hustling 8-ball pool at the seaside resort, Bundoran.

Depending on our success, we either slept in a £10 B&B or in a sea-facing golf hut at The Great Northern Hotel. On stormy nights, gaps in the vertical timbers let howling Atlantic winds blow through our bones.

We washed at the public swimming pool complex and hung out at a main street restaurant at the beginning and end of every day. There we stashed our sleeping bags and holdalls containing the few clothes we had, with an Omagh friend who worked and lodged there.

After seeing me bedraggled there one morning, a family friend sent her son to the restaurant to bring us back to their caravan, and gave us breakfast and a bed for a mid-morning sleep; a treat that continued for the duration of that family's summer holiday.

She was concerned about the damage that I was doing to my already fragile health.

I took a bus to Omagh and signed on the dole every two weeks, rather than one, due to being on holiday and therefore unavailable to sign weekly. I would then cash the cheque from the previous two weeks, sent to John Street in my absence, and head straight back to Bundoran.

On one such visit I was directed to the local Jobs Centre, where I was offered a job as a 'trainee joiner'. It was August 1980 and I knew that I had to get on with my life. So, I swapped the *craic* and the girls in Bundoran, and the UB40, for a job in a kitchen factory where they used me as a labourer and paid me as a trainee.

The money I had lent earlier that year to Casper would have paid me for four months.

At the factory, I spent the day standing in front of a four-foot-wide horizontal drill-head that bored holes into the sides of sheets of wood. In a monotonous routine, a forklift truck delivered panels of soon-to-be kitchen shelves and uprights, which I first lifted onto the drilling machine and then onto an empty pallet to be forklifted away.

Every evening, I prepared my lunch box for the following day at the factory and stumbled to bed, exhausted.

It was a Friday morning in early September, after only one

month at the factory, when I was working alongside another operative on a six-foot-wide machine that required two pairs of hands. As I leaned forward to adjust my side of the panel, my colleague depressed the foot clamp and a beer-bottle-sized wedge crushed the index finger of my right hand.

I could see through the separated flesh the bright white tip of my finger bone, and was driven off to the treatment room at Omagh Health Centre in the Chief Executive's Jaguar.

I never went back to the factory. The crushed finger proved to be the best thing that had happened to me in years.

On the way home, I passed the DHSS office where, until recently, I had signed on the dole, and saw the buildings of Omagh Tech in front of me. In the two-minute walk that followed, I decided to go back to school.

Arriving in the college foyer that morning, I had no idea what I might say or study. I asked to see the teacher who had brought me The City & Guilds exam papers in hospital fifteen months before, explained that I had left work, and would like to return to school to sit GCSEs.

He was supportive and summoned the Vice Principal, who said that the GCSE course had started a week before and that, in any event, a scholarship grant would have to be secured from the Western Education and Library Board before I could be considered for the course.

'I've been to grammar school,' I said. 'I'm smart. I will pass the exams, I won't let you down,' I pleaded.

I waited and watched through the glass pane of the school's office as the Vice Principal engaged in an extended telephone conversation with the Western Education and Library Board. He emerged fifteen minutes later with the news. They would take a chance; I could start Monday morning.

It was another good Friday.

CHAPTER TWELVE

Back Door to University

'As one of the few people here with qualifications,' I intoned, to laughter from my student peers, 'I do not think it is necessary to aspire to go to university to achieve academic fulfilment.'

My words, including the ironic opening line – referencing my City & Guilds Craft Certificate in Carpentry & Joinery, and rubbish GCSE grades – were meant to amuse. I was opening a debate between Omagh Tech and senior girls from the town's Loreto Convent Grammar School, a place Mum had attended forty years before.

The subject was: 'The role of education in Social Mobility.' I was studying sociology for the first time and had learned about concepts like Social Darwinism—the survival of the fittest—a metaphor for life to which I fully subscribed.

We discussed in class whether the notion of The American Dream still applied and whether it was possible to achieve economic and social success through sheer hard work—the *log cabin to the White House*, as my tutor said rhetorically.

I had not read a book since Walter Macken's *Seek the Fair Land* from my grammar school reading list, when I learned of how Oliver Cromwell had driven the Irish towards the Atlantic in pursuit of his 'To Hell or to Connaught' solution to the Irish Catholic problem, but was soon captivated by an amusing title from the English reading list: George Orwell's *Animal Farm*, a brilliant parody of a social order in society—the survival of the fittest.

The book ended with a message that I would relate to many times in the years that followed: *All animals are equal, but some are more equal than others.*

In the debate, my words were delivered with extra passion as I was following a haughty, highly-educated Loreto sixth-form girl, who asserted that the Business Education Council (BEC), National Diploma my sixteen-strong cohort was studying, was a 'back door to university'!

I had joined the BEC group with the worst qualifications and had never considered going to university. Many of my classmates intended to use the business studies training to embark on careers in accountancy or legal departments, but I wanted to learn skills that would help me run the family business, which I had now taken over.

Still, the 'back door to university' comment grated.

'The BEC course,' I said, 'was an alternative, intellectual challenge to the boringly predictable structures of mainstream education, which offered ready-made career options to successful students. Moreover, it offered drop-outs from mainstream education—people like me—a chance to return to a more suitable and fulfilling education than that offered by university.'

I was studying business to help with my real-life needs. University didn't come into it.

On my return to education a year before, a five-subject GCSE course had been cobbled together for me, comprising English Language, Mathematics, Physics with Chemistry, Geometrical Drawing and Building Construction.

The latter two subjects were a step up from my City & Guilds course, but the others presented an entirely different challenge. I had not studied in years, while most of my GCSE classmates were repeating subjects they had recently studied at other schools.

I was seventeen and initially shy about my situation; I didn't want to talk about my wasted years. But that added to the mystery and kept my name circulating in the chat amongst my new female friends. They wanted to know about the mystery and history, about what I'd been doing in the lost years since I left the Christian Brothers' Grammar School.

For the first time since primary school, I was motivated to learn, but found it difficult to return to the 'process' of education. Just like grammar school, one needed structure, and I had none. The concept of study was alien.

Fearing I might flop the New Year class tests I decided to prepare for them in earnest. During the days between Christmas and New Year, I laid all the coursework books on the huge oak table in the sitting room above the pub, while my parents, JFK, Pope Paul and the Mona Lisa looked down on me.

Later, when expressing satisfaction at my performance in the class test, my normally sardonic Mathematics tutor gave me a clear mandate to continue.

'You can do it, because you understand it,' he said.

Amongst the lecturers and students at Omagh Tech, I again found the intellectual stimulation of which I had been deprived since the wonderful Brother O'Reilly at primary school.

I was back in the education groove and enjoyed fantastic relationships with tutors and classmates. I struggled through the GCSE exams, and when they were over felt a degree of sangfroid and scolded myself that I should have done better.

The minimum entry requirement for the BEC business studies course was four GCSE grade C passes, which I was hopeful of achieving from the five exams taken.

When the results came through, I was about to embark on a

trip to Europe with a friend who worked for an international road haulier. We set off from Omagh at five am for a one-thousand-mile road trip, and the cab of the transport lorry was our home for the next four days.

Even though we couldn't speak any French our destination was the South of France, where we would spend a week camping in the sun.

On the way, we collected a consignment of beef at London's Smithfield Market, which we delivered to Paris' *Marché International de Rungis*, the world's largest wholesale food market.

We then continued along the Route du Soleil, past Lyon, and finally on to Toulon, where my friend and I separated from the driver and hitchhiked with our tents on our backs to a campsite at the nearby Hyères.

In London, we had waited at a twenty-four-hour café for a four am pick-up of meat at Smithfield Market.

It was impossible to imagine then that two decades later I would work at the Merrill Lynch Financial Centre, a few hundred metres away at King Edward Street, St. Paul's, or that I would retire from The City as a Merrill Lynch Managing Director and Country Manager for Ireland.

On that day, I reached into my pocket to marvel again at the crumpled slip of paper that listed my GCSE exam results. They read:

Building Construction	Grade C
English Language	Grade B
Geometrical Drawing	Grade C
Mathematics	Grade C
Physics with Chemistry	Grade D

Eighteen months later, around the time of my twentieth birthday, a tutor handed me a university application form and instructed me to complete it quickly, as the closure date was nearing.

I was then a keen follower of Thatcherism and Reaganomics and had a good grasp of the monetarist principles they advocated, so decided that Economics would be a good subject to study.

At the end of the first year of the BEC course, I had added Accountancy and Sociology to my GCSE roster, which now read one A, one B and four Cs.

With those grades, I knew there was no point in applying to Oxbridge but selected the grand-sounding London School of Economics, from which Mick Jagger had dropped out, Liverpool's John Moores University and, as my first choice, Belfast's Queen's University.

When the BEC course concluded six months later, I was one of only three from the sixteen-person group to achieve a distinction, and the only one to be admitted to Queen's.

At my final interview, Victor Hewitt, a senior economics lecturer, remarked that I had received a tremendous reference from Omagh Tech, and that had strongly influenced their decision to offer me a place.

After five barren years at grammar and secondary school, I found myself at Northern Ireland's premier university and, despite my circuitous route, had arrived there only one year behind many of my former Christian Brothers classmates.

I had been transported from the shop floor of the kitchen factory to the marbled halls of Queen's University, and no one was more surprised than me.

CHAPTER THIRTEEN

Drowned by the River

'What are you doing here?' I said to my old St Pat's Headmaster, Donal Donnelly, when I bumped into him in the foyer of the Queen's University Students' Union.

'I could ask you the same question,' he replied with a loud laugh.

I was in my third and final year of study at Queen's and we both knew that it was something of a miracle that I was there at all.

He had been a life-long advocate of education, and now, in his mid-fifties, had begun a master's degree course at Queen's. I joined him for lunch at the Union dining room, where he told me about his struggle to encourage pupils to attend secondary school, after the leaving age was raised from fifteen to sixteen in the early 1970s.

The non-participation of my brothers and I was not unique to us.

As we left the dining room at the Union, I showed him a nearby seating area where I regularly played evening poker with other students.

I had recently won my first 'Poker Classic' tournament at an Omagh social club where, for an entry fee of £20 I collected the winner's prize of £400.

I attributed that success to my skill at *Texas Holdem*, a

game that allowed an aggressive player to dominate the betting and seek to outmuscle others. Opponents needed to believe you were brave enough, or mad enough, to keep raising the betting stakes.

In the game, each player is dealt two cards to their hand, and another five cards that are communal to all players, are placed face down in the middle of the table.

The winner will be the player who can form the best five-card hand from the two in his hand, plus any three of the five-shared cards; or the player who can out-bet the opposition before all five mutual cards are turned.

The night after my triumph at Omagh, the poker stakes were raised considerably at a Portadown tournament. There, the entry fee was £100 for a prize of £3,000 and I took my place on one of the seven tables of seven players. I played extra aggressively and was soon knocked out, but was happy to leave behind the plastic chips to find a seat at one of the big cash games, which would start just as soon as a cohort of players exited the tournament game.

In the cash game, it was not long before my starting fund of £300 turned into £900, which I stacked in front of me in ten, twenty and fifty-pound notes. As more of the big money players joined the cash game, the stakes went higher, until my £900 was the price of playing one game.

My poker face was firm as I was dealt two aces in my hand and bet big before the Ace of Spades was turned face-up in the three-card *Flop*. My confidence was high and I determined to push the stakes higher and higher during the three remaining betting opportunities.

I did so again after the fourth card turned was revealed as another Spade, which almost certainly boosted the chances of one of my opponents filling an ace-high flush of Spades.

As we approached the River card, I knew that my three aces were still the best hand, as my opponents needed to turn one more Spade to beat me. Any of them with two spades in their hand would 'potentially' have nine more still to play for; at best, a one-in-six chance.

Alternatively, they may have had two of a pair in their hand and with no pairs on the table, the best hand possible was three of a kind. As things stood my three Aces was the winning hand.

I could not lose without one of the others catching another Spade or a card to make a pair with one of the four already turned. The latter would give me a pretty unassailable 'Ace's up' (three Aces plus the pair), which could only be trumped by the highly improbable chance that my opponent had the same pair in his hand, to give him poker-fours.

Meanwhile, another Ace to go with the two in my hand, and the Ace of Spades from the earlier three-card Flop, would give me an unbeatable four-Aces.

I made the maximum bet allowed: half the pot - £400.

This play was designed to scare off the bookie and other players, to make the bookie fold in case my hand of cards did not improve.

With £1,200 in cash now on the table, it was the biggest pot of the night, and two players dropped out.

It was just the bookie and me as a crowd of spectators gathered for the shoot-out, circling the table like Apaches at Little Bighorn. Tensions were already high between the bookie and me as he too was an aggressive player.

'I'll match your £400 and raise you £800,' said my enemy, as he placed twelve one-hundred-pound stacks on the table.

'£300 is all I have left,' I countered.

'The bet is £800,' he fired back, pointedly. 'Match the bet or fold.'

'It's table stakes,' I retorted, 'and £300 is what I have left on the table. You cannot bet me out of the game. Call the referee if you like.'

He was forced to withdraw five of his twelve hundred-pound stacks, as I gathered the three hundred pounds in cash before me and waited.

'£2,200 it is then, I'm all in,' I said and fired my three folded bundles of notes onto the table.

The pot was now equivalent to more than two years of my annual university maintenance grant. No sooner had the words left my mouth than my opponent scrambled to flip the River card to end the game.

There would be no more betting, as all my funds were exhausted and I watched and sank as the four of Spades emerged on the table.

'An Ace-high flush of Spades,' blustered the bookie, almost unable to contain himself as he laid two Spade-suited cards next to the three Spades that lay side by side on the table. With no pair among the five cards that lay face up on the table, and no Spades in my hand, he won.

The River had saved him and drowned me.

I was broke and had plenty of time to muse about what might have been, as I had to hang around until the small hours awaiting a lift to Belfast with an experienced player I knew from the poker tournament circuit.

Weeks before, during another Sunday night game at an Omagh hotel, my regular playing mates had been raided by armed robbers. We regularly hired a private room at the hotel for a cash-only game, but I had returned to Belfast that evening.

The gunman forced my poker friends to lay face down on the floor as the cash from the poker table was swept into a black bin liner. Each attendee was then forced to empty their pockets of cash, and one non-playing observer faced the wrath of an angry gunman when the linings of his pockets proved to be empty.

'Maybe it's just as well you lost that hand,' said my driver.

'We may not have got out of there safely tonight.'

By then I had secured a job offer with the international accountancy firm, Deloitte, subject only to attaining the BSc in Economics with Accountancy for which I was studying. Luckily for me, no final exam grade was targeted.

In the second-year exams, I had achieved two 2:1s and a 2:2 in the three exams and aimed to achieve an overall 2:1 grade. To do so, I only needed to secure four more 2:1 results from the six remaining modules.

Learning at Queen's had not been any more difficult than learning at Omagh Tech. It had been a huge intellectual leap to study advanced statistical theories like Least Squares Regression Line, standard deviations, binomial distributions, and random walks, but not more difficult.

My plan was to study after St Patrick's Day, March 17, 1986. In an approach that I had adopted for every exam since going back to school six years before, that would give me two months to cram the necessary work before the exams began.

I was living in a dingy flat in Fitzroy Avenue, near Queen's. We had three bedrooms in the second-floor attic space that were warmed by electric bar-heaters. So cold was the large first-floor living room that it was no surprise to learn that the previous residents had taken out most of the banisters to use as firewood.

My flatmates attended the University of Ulster at Jordanstown and all three of us were studying flat-out. For the first time in my three years at college, I was attending the Queen's Library for reasons other than photocopying.

I went into the library early and came out late, and halfway through my six-part final exams I realised that there was a real risk that my plans could fall apart. Was it possible to transcribe all the copied notes, which occupied a greater proportion of my study files than my own?

While I could readily grasp economic theory, I found myself in European Economics being asked to describe elements of the Treaty of Rome, the treaty that established what would later become the European Union, about which I knew nothing.

In Financial Accounting, I was about to face subjects like 'Accounting for Leasing', the interpretation of which could not be achieved without study.

I was putting in twenty-hour days, seven days a week, burning the midnight oil, and it was taking its toll. I was physically and mentally shattered. Expectation added to the pressure.

I had done it all. I had gone back to school and made it to the top university, the only one in my family to do so. It grieved me to think that I was about to let down myself and everyone else.

Fortunately, three of the four Economics exams had come first, and I did well in them, although they consumed my study time and the inevitable end came when I attended the Financial Accounting exam.

It was a subject with which I should have had little difficulty, but I knew going into what was intended to be a three-hour exam that I didn't know even half the coursework. I went along in the hope that I might find something to answer—something that might allow me to scrape through.

That hope quickly evaporated and I found myself idling at my exam desk. More than thirty minutes after I had taken my seat in the giant student union canteen, I had written nothing on the test paper except my name and college number.

There were many different exams going on, and in a row next to me, I saw a group of students prepare to hand in their papers. Their exit was exactly one hour after I had begun to attempt the Financial Accounting exam, and as they stood and headed for the door, I ghosted out of my chair and left too.

'I see you left with the engineers,' droned one college friend later. All I could do was laugh with him.

I knew that I would suffer a similar fate with the forthcoming European Economics and Management Accountancy exams and raised the white flag. I could take no more. I could not sit the exams. I could not learn a year's work in a few days, especially in the mental state to which I had descended.

Later that day, the doorbell rang at my flat. At first, I dared not look out the window for fear of seeing a fellow student intending to console me. No amount of sympathy was going to help fix the situation.

But when I heard a voice shout my name from the street below, I looked out and saw my economics lecturer, Victor Hewitt, standing beside his BMW on the roadside. He had found my address from college records. He whisked me off to the medical centre, where I was declared unfit to sit any more exams.

A few weeks later, I sat and passed the European Economics exam in a quiet room at the college administration office and, with the failed Financial Accounting and un-sat Management Accounting, was awarded a Pass Degree.

I was very lucky, and was soon set to start work at Deloitte, where my hopes of achieving an accountancy qualification quickly faded. The prospect of another five-years' study did not appeal, and so bad was the wage that I raged internally on receipt of the after-tax pay slip of £268 per month.

I had won and lost more on the flip of a single poker card.

Working there was the equivalent of taking on a vocation; having declined the priesthood, accountancy was not for me.

Throughout my life to date, I had been known to all as Christy, a name given to me at the pub. 'Ah Christy Ring,' said one old customer referencing the Cork hurling legend and the name stuck until I was twenty-three-years-old.

'Christy makes it too easy for you to be identified as a Catholic - from now on you're Chris!' said a fellow-Catholic boss at Deloitte in Belfast; important in a city where you could die for being in the wrong place with the wrong name.

I returned to Queen's to take part in the annual graduate recruitment fair—the *milk round* of 1987. My continued interest in the stock market led me to a Dublin-based recruitment agent who arranged an interview with the Ulster Investment Bank (UIB).

They were impressed by my success at 'stagging', buying and quickly selling again shares in the newly privatised UK state companies; BT, TSB and British Gas, where the Thatcher Government's 'wider share ownership' policy was championed by the 'tell Sid' advertising campaign.

I started work in the UIB dealing room in Dublin just seven weeks before the infamous *Black Monday*, October 19, 1987, when the Dow Jones Index tumbled.

As trillions were wiped off the value of stock markets around the world, I stood behind colleagues huddled over video screens and watched share prices plunge.

I didn't know the significance of what was unfolding before me, but the fear and panic among my asset manager colleagues was palpable, as the Dow suffered its biggest ever same-day crash, a fall of 22.6%.

It was a sea of red. 'What shall we do,' asked the hovering bosses; 'buy or sell?' I didn't know the answer but was excited by the question. *I could do that*, I thought.

PART THREE

Justice

Graduation from Queen's University, Economics
with Accountancy – 1986, aged 23

CHAPTER FOURTEEN

What Do You Say to Someone Who Saved Your Life?

WPC Colleen McMurray, the investigating officer, and a male colleague came to see me in my final days at the Ulster Hospital. I was resting on top of my bed, with my fixator supported by a pillow, as they approached.

'The last woman who came to see me fainted!' I said, seeking to break her gaze.

'No, no,' she replied, assuredly. 'I was just thinking how well you've done since I saw you in ICU a few weeks ago.'

'I don't remember that.'

'We thought it better to give you some time to recover,' she replied, and took a seat by my bedside. 'What do you remember of the crash?' she continued after some small talk.

I had thought a lot about the crash following the visit of my friends from Dublin, and was particularly struck by one reference to the 'great big hole in the hedge' caused by the lorry careering into a field on my side of the road.

'Nothing. I remember nothing at all about the crash,' I said slowly, as I dug deep into my memory. 'I remember getting petrol on my way into Newry that morning, but nothing about the crash itself. I went to the cinema with my girlfriend the night before. What about the lorry driver? What does he say happened?' The latter words spurted out as I looked for answers of my own.

'We hope to get a statement from him shortly.'

'You know he hasn't been here to see me and has made no contact with my family,' I said, as the tears welling in my eyes ran down my face, making the WPC spring to her feet.

'Are you okay, Christopher? I don't want to distress you,' she said.

'I'm sorry, that came from nowhere.' My head was spinning. I did not have a clue what had happened. 'What about the nurse who saved my life? What does she say happened?'

'Her father has called me regularly, asking about you, but they didn't see the accident,' she said, as she and her colleague made their way away from my bed.

The WPC had been kind and considerate, but my antenna was flashing red. I was no longer happy to be blamed for the crash.

Where was the absent lorry driver? Why had he not come to see me or even contacted my family?

From the moment I had woken in hospital, I had been told that the police were sure that I had been at fault, and accepted that to be true. That had helped with my recovery, as I had no one to blame but myself. But everything had changed.

I knew that I needed to rebuild my strength, and was thankful that the gash to my shin had not resulted in a fracture. Without the ability of my arms to hold crutches, a broken leg would have confined me to bed for months.

With my lower limbs still intact, I tramped the corridors, shuffling from ward to ward, adding extra distance every day. Impressed by my fortitude, the nursing staff of the neighbouring geriatric ward pointed to an old lady recovering from an operation who had not yet managed to get back on her feet.

'Would you speak with her?' said one. 'She needs to believe that she can do it.'

The lady sat stooped forward, leaning on a Zimmer frame,

in a high, firm, chair. I crouched towards her and talked through my wired teeth.

'The nurses tell me that your hip replacement operation went well,' I said, as she leaned back and looked at me—a stranger.

'Yes,' she said. 'They say that, but I'm still very sore.'

'Look at me,' I said, observing her reaction as she focused on my ravaged face. 'I promise you that everything will get better once you get back on your feet. You can do it.'

'I will try,' she said.

The next day, she did.

Soon the paraphernalia attached to my body would be removed. Following an injection of local anaesthetic in my left hand, Mr. Hart made a small incision that revealed the steel base of the K-wire, which was quickly yanked with tweezers through the bones in my hand. The surgeon explained that some loss of bone from the outside metacarpal meant that the little finger would now be permanently drawn away from the others.

Removing the wires from my jaw was less straightforward. Mr. Ramsey-Baggs applied maybe twenty numbing injections to the gums above and below where the wires nestled between my teeth. The wires were then wrenched out with surgical pliers.

At first, my mouth opening was only enough to insert the base of the uninjured forefinger or thumb of my left hand. They were the only moving limbs above my waist that still functioned as before, and in the weeks that followed, would form a wedge to slowly prise the jaw apart.

When, finally, Mr. Macafee removed the right-angled frame of the fixator and unscrewed from my bones the four pins that had kept it in place, the arm flopped free, feather light and unwieldy.

The Humpty Dumpty Man was free to go home.

The family home was no longer the stinking hovel above the pub, and the family included our stepfather, Paddy, by whom we had not been adopted.

He was a large man with a happy smile and huge, incongruous hands, the fingertips of which had been deformed as a baby when he crawled into a tray of hot ashes. He was naturally left-handed – or, in the local vernacular, kitter-handed, from the Gaelic word *citog* – and received many beatings as a schoolboy to correct the 'deficiency'.

In his early fifties he had been struck by a major heart attack three weeks before Mum died, and for a time they lay in adjacent wards at Omagh's County Hospital before she was transferred to the General Hospital for her final days.

I was six years old when he married our mother, and Martin's early closeness with him, running errands and being his apprentice at a workbench constructed in an outhouse, led to Paul calling him the 'blue-eyed-boy,' a cause of much annoyance, as we all three boys had blue eyes.

From wooden battens they made a new *KATE'S Bar* sign for the pub, with the S constructed from several parts, and hauled flat stones from Dunfanaghy to replace the polished black marble panels and silver *McGale's* sign from Dad's pub.

But I was one of the McGales of John Street and, like Paul, had no desire for a father figure. In a fit of rage at Dublin Zoo a year into the marriage, I refused to get into the packed estate wagon, and as the car slowly moved off, fired a fistful of roadside grit and pebbles at the vehicle, with the words, 'You're not my father.'

After Mum's death, and his cardiac arrest, when he was fifty-two and I was twelve, for maybe a year we sat for hours in her bedroom at opposite ends of templates, building circular flowerpot stands and crucifixes from glued lollypop sticks, exercises that improved his wobbly kitter-hand, and added to my stash of cash from sales to visitors and pub customers.

By the time I was eighteen, in early 1981, I had taken over the running of the family business a few months after I had gone back to school at Omagh Tech.

The business had been in steady decline in the six years since Mum's death, when the family was called together for the reading of her Will, an event we had understood would happen at Joanie's eighteenth birthday, still four years away.

Having been outside the business since I went to hospital with TB, I was delighted to know that I now owned one-eighth of the assets in Omagh and Dunfanaghy, along with my siblings and Paddy. But, as it turned out, I also owned one-eighth of the liabilities.

The trustees revealed that they had called us together because AIB Bank were calling for a change of management due to trading losses at the pub, and at a restaurant Mum had developed to provide a role in the business for Paddy, and the lack of income being achieved from rented properties.

I was not alone at feeling anger at the situation. We had lost our mother and were now losing her business, and no-one seemed to have any suggestions as to how we could fix the problem.

'Someone,' said Mum's solicitor and trustee, Jim Montague, 'will have to join me at a meeting with AIB,' and after the momentary vacuum that followed, said, 'Christopher, you're doing mathematics at school, aren't you? Will you do it?'

I wanted to make the decisions. I shut and sold the restaurant, sold the next-door grocery store to the tenant, and extracted more rent from Dad's brother Arthur for the outhouses he used for storage at the back of the pub.

Mum had always said that 'the customer is always right', but when I took over behind the bar and closed the credit book, I faced the inevitable wrath of pub regulars.

The changes meant there was no work at home for Paddy, Martin, and Paul. Marie and Noelle were both married and away, and Briegie and Joanie lived above the pub with Paddy, Martin and me. For months afterwards Martin sat on the living room sofa reading books, and I remember him laugh his way through the *Don Quixote de La Mancha* tome, about the escapades of the Knight errant and his squire, Sancho Panza.

The girls were still at school and I would complete my GCSE year while running the pub.

Weddings or funerals were the only time we all got together after that, and one such occasion was the wake and funeral three years later of Mum's brother Francie, in October 1984.

'Martin should be running the pub,' said Uncle Mick pointedly as we stood by the Aga range cooker in Granny's kitchen the night before the funeral, when I explained that I was travelling back and forth between Omagh and Belfast by bus and that it was taking its toll on my study life.

I replied that the bank would not accept anyone other than me being responsible for the business's debt, and suggested that the only way it could be done was for Martin to buy the current stock, assume the liabilities owed to drinks suppliers, and HMRC, and then take over by renting the pub from the business.

'That would cost about £20,000,' I said, 'and there's more than that owed to AIB.'

'Okay,' he said. 'I'll give you the twenty thousand.'

'Not me,' I said, 'Martin!'

Two months later, on December 21, 1984, in return for Martin's annual rental of £7,800, I swapped the Christopher J. McGale trading as Kate's Bar A/c for a £27,000 term loan at AIB. At that rate, the total debt would be eliminated in a few years.

With the business on the road to recovery, I took Paddy

to a local car showroom and bought a new £5,000 Volvo hatchback.

At the same time, with the aid of an Urban Development Grant, I had drawn up plans to convert our old beer store on Church Hill into a townhouse for the family, funded by converting our living area above the pub into five lettable bedsits.

In his early sixties, Paddy was not entirely sure about the changes, and in an emotional moment asked if I was 'pushing him out.' But it was not long before he was poring over the plans and became an auxiliary foreman on the Church Hill building site.

He loved his new home, outside which was parked a new car to drive with Briegie and Joanie to their beloved Dunfanaghy. There he would sit in the parked car in the village square and *Céilí* with the locals, and such was his popularity that at the 1986 village festival they awarded him the honorary title of Lord Mayor of Dunfanaghy. The offer of a million pounds would not have made him happier.

In early December 1988, two weeks after my release from hospital, and two months after my devastation, I persuaded a reluctant Paddy to take me to the crash scene.

On the way, we visited my Renault 5 at a scrap yard in Camlough, Co Armagh.

The car and I had been dissected diagonally by the lorry's cutting wheel that swept over me from my right side. The area behind me and all the way around to the front grill on the passenger's side remained intact.

Inside the car, I observed that the clock on the dashboard had stopped at 6.35am.

The shirts that had previously hung, freshly ironed, on a hook above the rear passenger window lay in a twisted mound on the back seat like a papier-mâché sculpture, caked in my hardened blood.

A pool of dried blood was spread all over the back seat and the driver's seatbelt was torn and ragged. That belt had saved my life.

We didn't know exactly where I had crashed, and Paddy, normally a slow driver, had now become even slower as we passed the last of the landmarks indicated to us by Fergus Cosgrove as markers for his home.

We passed a landmark at the brow of the hill that we had been ascending for some time. After that, we were to follow downhill towards the petrol station, and take the first right-hand turn into the driveway of his bungalow that looked over the road from on high.

What do you say to someone who saved your life? I thought, as we approached the crash scene, a stretch of road on the A1 at Killeen, outside Newry. Not a word was spoken as we slowly drove the remaining few hundred metres.

On my left I saw the 'great big hole in the hedge' that my joking hospital visitor had referenced, where the DAF truck and its twenty-tonne load had careered off the road, across a ditch, and down a steep decline into a boggy field below.

The lorry was gone but its wheels had dug a path through the field that was still visible seven weeks after the crash.

In front, spread across the road, were scrape marks delineating the point of impact. Large circular scrapes were hewn into the tarmac surface over which we drove.

We took our place in the middle of the road and waited to make the right-hand turn into the driveway of the Cosgrove family's home. Cars and lorries sped past from in front and behind, left and right, making our car tremble like it was in a wind tunnel.

It was easy to see how you might crash there; how you might die there.

As we waited to cross the oncoming traffic, I saw on the hard shoulder a soot-like, blackened area of debris taking the shape of my car—the place where Karen Cosgrove had saved my life.

I fiddled with a gift-wrapped bottle of perfume, an inadequate gift I had bought for her at an Omagh pharmacy that morning. Had I made a big enough effort? I was nervous.

The icy ground glistened as we drove up the lane towards the house and the traffic hurtled by on the A1 road below.

'I see you brought the steering wheel with you,' said the waiting Fergus, as he opened the passenger door for me, 'and the number plate too.' He pointed at the items on the back seat of the car.

'Yes, souvenirs,' I replied, as I offered my right hand to Fergus. The hand was bound in a tan-coloured, Velcro-sealed, synthetic brace, that contained a steel insert that ran from the middle of my hand to halfway up my forearm, to keep the wrist upright.

'Thank you so much for your help,' I added, fighting to hold back tears.

I had not left the warmth and comfort of the Church Hill town house and Paddy's blazing fire in the weeks since I returned from hospital, and felt nervous about falling on the icy surface.

At home, to protect myself from a fall, I had developed a routine of reversing my way up the short winding stairs that led to our first-floor bedrooms and bathroom. That way I would fall onto my backside should I need to and would not hurt my arms.

As I stepped from the car, I saw that the windows at the front of the hilltop bungalow were boarded with timber panels, awaiting repair from damage sustained from a 1,000-pound culvert bomb that had killed Robin and Pauline Hanna and their youngest son, David, five months before. The IRA had mistaken their car for that of a High Court Judge.

A year before that, a bomb placed nearby in a roadside

parked car had taken the lives of Lord Justice Maurice Gibson and his wife Cecily, and ended the rugby career of Ireland International, Nigel Carr, who was travelling with two International colleagues in the opposite direction on their way to attend training in Dublin.

Fergus offered his left arm as a crutch and led us around the back of his bungalow towards a timber ramp that led to the family's kitchen. The ramp was icy too and I instinctively turned around, edging up backwards so I could use the fingers of my splinted right hand to hold onto the single handrail and could drop onto my bottom in the event of slipping.

'You poor lad,' said Fergus, when I turned to make my way into his kitchen.

'It's okay. I'm just making sure that I don't hurt my arms.'

I could see his look of helplessness as I slipped out of my jacket, edging it off my right shoulder, then my left, as if I was slipping out of a straitjacket in the manner of Harry Houdini.

At that moment, words that I had not expected to hear came from Fergus's mouth. 'There is no way that you caused that accident. The lorry ended up on your side of the road and so did you. The driver was probably mooching for cigarettes in his glove compartment or fiddling with his tachograph when he clipped the cornerstone of my garden wall, ran right over you and finished up in that field across the road,' he concluded, pointing in the direction of the field and the gap in the hedge that the lorry had careered through.

As we examined the scene, Karen emerged from another room. I had learned from Fergus that she was soon to be married and felt even more awkward about the perfume I had brought as thanks.

'It was dark, and I was getting up for work that morning when I heard the bang,' said Karen, an eighteen-year-old trainee nurse at Newry's Daisy Hill Hospital. 'At first, we thought it was another bomb, until we saw the lorry's lights in the field across the road, and your car opposite the driveway.'

'The car was smoking. I was worried that it might explode. I was worried about Karen,' said Fergus.

We talked no more about the accident. It was time to talk about Karen's forthcoming wedding. What do you say to someone who saved your life? Words are not enough.

Karen had staunched the flow of blood on which I was choking with the mound of shirts that remained on the car's back seat. Without that help, I would have died.

In that smoking car, she had risked her life to save the life of a stranger.

CHAPTER FIFTEEN

Rehab

What am I doing here? I thought.

I had lost my right elbow, nearly lost my arm and both hands. Red, linear scars tracked the openings where titanium screws were inserted to hold my left arm together. The mark of a lorry's wheelrim ran down my face and neck.

It was a quarter-to-ten in the morning on the first Monday of January 1989, about twelve weeks after the accident. I was looking at the reflected image in the wire-glass window of the manager's office at the Joss Cardwell Rehabilitation Unit on Belfast's Holywood Road. On the other side of the glass, patients had gathered in the breakfast area for 10am therapy sessions.

I could see injured people of all ages and sexes: in wheelchairs, on crutches, without limbs, with horrible burns, dragging one side of their body and just shuffling—everyone moving slowly, victims of The Troubles, of strokes, of fires, and road traffic accidents like me.

Victims everywhere.

I looked again at myself in the reflected glass and thought: Surely, I'm not as bad as that?

The day had started badly. Around half-an-hour earlier, an NHS minibus driver had rung the doorbell of the house that my college girlfriend shared with others in the student area of

Belfast, where I planned to stay for the duration of my rehab.

After readying me for the day, she had left for work with her flatmates. I sat alone adorned in the grey tracksuit that would be my daily garb in the months ahead.

'Push the door,' I said from the inside, through the frosted glass panel of the front door. 'Push the door,' I repeated.

'Do what?' he replied through the letterbox.

To open the door, I had supported the splinted wrist of my right hand, cupped between the thumb and forefinger of my left, and turned the lock anticlockwise, but I could not pull the door towards me. I could not break the airlock of the draft-proofed front door.

'Push the door,' I said again, crossly, until finally the door opened to the sound of a puff of air.

The driver locked the door and gave the key to me, before ushering me through the double doors of the NHS minibus that would ferry me and others to rehab.

I was in no mood to talk with an elderly nun who was helped along the aisle into the seat opposite me, and even less with a cheery chap who limped onto the bus wearing bedroom slippers, a tee shirt and boxer shorts, out of which bulged his manhood.

'Hello son,' said the nun.

'Hello Sister,' I replied. She was a tiny lady, no more than five-foot tall, and I learned that she had been hit by a car while on a pedestrian crossing and needed to rebuild her confidence.

I had signed up for physiotherapy not psychoanalysis, I thought, reflecting on my fellow travellers whose afflictions appeared to be more psychological than physical. This was not what I had been looking forward to.

At the rehab centre, I was instructed to wait alone in the minibus while the driver went to fetch a member of staff. Then a towering nurse approached, dressed in a white pinafore, navy blue slacks and black shoes, and helped me out of the vehicle and led me into the building.

Everyone looked up from the plastic canteen chairs and wheelchairs as the nurse and the new boy entered the building.

'Are you okay, Christopher?' she asked, as I took a seat against a wall in her office.

'Yes, thank you.' I did not feel remotely okay.

'Can I get you something to help you relax?'

'No, thank you. I am relaxed,' I said firmly.

She left me alone in the office and promised to return with an itinerary for my day. I looked again through the wire-glass window of the manager's office at the occupants of the breakfast area and imagined the nurse returning with a thimble cup containing two small pink tablets.

It was like a scene from the movie, *One Flew Over the Cuckoo's Nest*. I smiled at the thought and awaited the return of my Nurse Ratchet.

Before going to rehab in Belfast, I had attended thrice-weekly sessions at the Physiotherapy Department at the Tyrone County Hospital in Omagh, where the ladies wrapped my arms in hot wax bandages, and we talked about Christmas shopping in Dublin.

There was a steady flow of visitors to the snug little house on Church Hill, where Paddy and I occupied both rooms. A fire blazed in the hearth of the imposing slate fireplace that had been transferred from the old sitting room in John Street.

Alongside the fireplace stood the huge antique side dresser, with the large inset mirror that also came from the big room above the pub.

A back boiler behind the glowing coal fire provided gallons of hot water for my daily baths, where the water's heat and buoyancy allowed me to stretch my physical limits, as I pulled and pushed one limb against another, before Paddy hauled me to my feet from behind.

Nurse Ratchet's itinerary for that day involved meetings with the resident General Practitioner, a clinical psychologist, and a physiotherapist, all of whom would assess me before my daily therapies began.

'How long do you think I'll have to come here?' I asked the GP.

'It's impossible to tell, but given the extent of your injuries nine, maybe twelve months.'

'But I'm not that bad!' I gasped. 'I have made huge progress.'

'Yes,' he replied, looking at me studiously. 'I am sure that you have made great progress, but these limbs don't move properly.'

He leant forward and lifted both my arms by the wrists.

'We may have to stiffen that wrist; arthritis,' he said, tapping his right index finger on the outside of my left hand. 'And we don't know if the radial nerve will ever allow your right wrist to function properly. You were lucky to keep the arm.'

He then placed his hands on both temples, as if to lock my head in place, and pressed his left thumb on my right cheekbone until it hurt. 'There's a fracture there,' he said, moving his thumb along a tingling nerve that ran to my upper lip. 'And this head injury will take time to recover,' he followed, placing an open hand over the long scar on the right side of my forehead. 'It's a shame I didn't see that swelling earlier, we could have started to reduce it by now.'

I raised my splinted hand and felt the golf-ball-sized lump on my forehead. It was sore to touch but was not among the things that I knew needed fixing.

'How can I reduce it?' I asked.

'You need to put pressure on it. I would have applied a cold steel plate, wrapped tightly in a crepe bandage. But it's probably too late now.'

For weeks afterwards, I would lean my head firmly onto the emulsion-painted walls of our Church Hill living room, until the pain and the swelling subsided.

'You know, Chris, you are very lucky to be here—lucky to be sitting here having this conversation. You have suffered immense physical damage and potentially a lot from that head injury too. But you're in the right place. We will measure it all and help you regain the most that is possible to regain. But it will be a long, hard road—a long, hard and painful road.'

The doctor then made me walk along a straight white line in the gymnasium, putting one foot in front of the other as a drunk driver might be asked to do by a police officer. I swayed from side-to-side and felt his hands on my shoulders as I lost my footing and tried to remain steady.

For the first time I became aware of my balance problem.

'The frontal lobe injury has led to slower movement and a permanent dragging on the left side of the body,' he observed. 'The symptoms are equivalent to those of a mild stroke,' he said, just as Mr. Macafee had. 'The perforated eardrum injury suggests trauma in the temporal lobe area. That might cause your emotions to cascade one way and another.'

I already knew exactly what he meant by cascading emotions.

'And I'll make an appointment for you with the Speech Therapy Department.'

'Why?'

'It's nothing too much to worry about. But we need to sharpen up those vowels.'

'Really?'

'It's probably a combination of things,' he said. 'The head injury, the contusion, the broken jaw, the perforation—they're all playing their part.'

Everything came as a surprise.

Years later I wondered whether I had been suffering from a form of dyspraxia at that time.

'Okay,' I said, resignedly.

My next appointment was with a clinical psychologist, who began the examination by giving me a word to remember for the day—China.

'You're serious? Remember China for the day?'

'Yes. We'll see.' She scowled back at me. 'Let's try some short-term recall,' she said, and asked me to repeat some numbers.

'One, three, five, seven, nine. No problem.'

'Okay, let's make it a bit harder,' she said, and proceeded to fire random numbers at me until my head felt quite scrambled by the pressure.

'Are we nearly done?' I said, hoping for respite.

'Would you like a glass of water?'

'No. I just want to get to the end of these tests.'

'We have lots more to do, but let me give you one more number test,' she replied.

'Subtract 7 from 100 as fast as you can.'

'7 from 100—is that what you want?' I said, stalling for time while already computing the numbers in my head.

'One hundred, ninety-three, eight-six, seventy-nine, seventy-two, sixty-five, fifty-eight, fifty-one, forty-four, thirty-seven, thirty, twenty-three, sixteen, nine and two,' I said in a flash. 'Is that what you are looking for?'

'Very good, the fastest I have ever seen,' she replied, almost smiling.

She then read from a short story and asked me about the characters. Who married whom? What was the daughter's name? There was no let-up, and I imagined myself answering questions against the clock on a television quiz show.

'Précis the following,' she said, as I listened hard, so I could repeat every word.

'Hold on,' I interjected, as the seconds wore on. 'How am I supposed to repeat all that?'

'Not repeat,' she said. 'Précis.'

And I did.

Remember China for the rest of the day. What was that all about? I pondered, as I sat at lunch. I was in a mild state of shock. My brain capacity had been stretched to the limit. I had passed the examination but felt totally defeated. What if I hadn't been able to answer the questions?

I had been one of the first to take a seat in the canteen that catered for patients and staff, and had finished lunch when a young man, who sat in a wheelchair across the table to my right, drew me into conversation.

He was in his early twenties and told me, through slurred words, that he had been asleep with his head resting against a rear window when the joy-rider car in which he was travelling crashed and hit a wall, fracturing his skull and impairing his 'cognitive function'.

He spoke with his head and neck cocked to one side, and despite his struggle for words, was enthusiastic and light-hearted. It was strange to hear someone use a medical term like 'cognitive function' through slurred speech.

Then a well-groomed, fifty-something lady in a flowery dress was helped into a chair opposite. She'd had a severe stroke and I watched as she attempted to feed lunch to herself with a plastic spoon. It was difficult for her to direct the food into her mouth and I was glad that I had finished eating.

Excruciating is the only word I could use to describe the physiotherapy sessions that followed lunch. The therapist pushed and pulled for maximum extension and contraction in my elbow-less right arm.

I lay on my back, shut my eyes, breathed deeply and grimaced as the physiotherapist steadily pushed my arm towards my head and then pulled it all the way back again towards her chest, until I could take no more.

That, along with the manipulation of my left hand, pronation, and supination, would be a daily ritual in the months that followed.

I often laughed exaggeratedly to relieve the pain, which prompted the chap in the boxer shorts to ask why I 'enjoyed it so much?'

It was not funny. I was patient number 890006, the sixth new patient of 1989. It was the biggest challenge of my life.

My girlfriend and I had been together four years, since our second year at university, and she had been a rock in the three months since my accident, visiting daily in hospital and travelling to Omagh every weekend. But I needed to be alone in this fight and, after a week in Belfast, I returned to Omagh and commuted daily.

Paddy had dinner ready on my return, just as he did every day in the months that followed. For weeks we lived on minced beef and mashed potatoes, as my stomach recovered from five weeks of food deprivation.

Looking in the mirror of the giant side dresser in the narrow townhouse, I hardly knew myself. My face was permanently covered in facial hair and I had lost 25% of my bodyweight, having gone from twelve stone in weight to nine.

One evening, while pounding the Gallows Hill streets to build strength, I met the teenage son of a pub-regular, whom I'd known since he was a child. As we passed one another on the narrow, street-lit footpath, I greeted him to no response. We continued in the opposite direction to one another until he called after me, 'Do I know you?'

Noelle came by in the mornings, plugged the perforation in my ear with Vaseline-coated cotton wool, and washed my hair with the bath's shower extension before I caught the ten-past-eight coach to Belfast every weekday.

I read an Irish Times newspaper en-route and, in the weeks that followed, felt my concentration return, and with it, the prospect of work.

On the first day that I travelled from Omagh to Belfast, I

caught a Citybus from The city centre to the rehab unit on the Holywood Road, and risked serious injury trying to find a seat on the moving vehicle.

I couldn't use the support straps that hung overhead—my arms and hands couldn't buffer my body weight when I was shunted forward—and my balance problems added to the general unsteadiness as I rocked and rolled down the aisle of the moving bus.

It was scary knowing that I couldn't protect myself as I bumped from seat to seat while seeking an empty one.

Later, before I returned to the Great Victoria Street Coach Station in another Citybus, I carefully uttered the following words for the first time: 'Excuse me driver, can you please wait until I sit down before you drive off. I'm handicapped.'

I had come a long way.

CHAPTER SIXTEEN

Back to Work

There was snow outside when WPC McMurray and a male RUC colleague visited me at Church Hill, soon after my December visit to the crash scene. Fergus Cosgrove's words about the likely cause of the crash were in my mind.

For security reasons, they travelled in an unmarked car and arrived unannounced. She found me wearing a round-necked, white tee shirt. In addition to my scarred face and neck, it revealed in all its glory the devastation to my hands, arms, and elbow, and highlighted the thinness of my body.

'What do you remember?' she asked me once again.

'I remember nothing, I'm afraid. Nothing.'

'What is the last thing that you remember before the crash?'

'I remember watching the movie *Amadeus* at the Ormeau Road cinema with my girlfriend the night before and getting petrol in Newry at a twenty-four-hour service station shortly before the crash. That's all.'

Sitting opposite me in the living room, she looked at her notebook. 'The other driver, Aidan Devlin, has made a detailed statement saying that he could not avoid you—that he pulled the lorry onto the hard shoulder trying to avoid you, but that the passenger side of the truck clipped the cornerstone of the garden wall, causing the lorry to crash into your car.'

My heart sank.

'I'm sorry, Christopher, but we can only go on the evidence that we are presented with,' she said softly, as if willing me to come up with something more.

The optimistic bubble, that had sustained me since my visit to the crash scene, burst. It dawned on me that I might face a criminal prosecution for having caused the crash and be charged with dangerous driving.

After a moment, I looked across at her and said, 'He never came to see me, you know. He nearly killed me, and he never came to see me.'

There was not a sound in the room except the crackling of coals burning in Paddy's open fire, until her male companion broke the silence. 'You're the guy that all the confusion was about at Newry RUC Station?'

'Yes, that's right,' I replied. 'They told my sister that I was dead.'

I stood up and sought to get a grip on my emotions. I looked back at the seated WPC and said, 'Look, I could lie to you. I could contradict what he said. I could say that I was on my own side of the road and wasn't aware of anything until he ran right over me. Even the man at the scene of the crash said that it was the lorry driver's fault, and that the police didn't arrive at the scene until three hours after the crash, when all the debris was spread everywhere. How can you determine anything?'

As the interview concluded, I made one further attempt to fend off a possible criminal charge. 'I have suffered enough, you know. It has been terrible.'

With that, they left.

By the spring of 1989, I had developed a perpetual routine of moving, twisting, and pushing my defective body parts to their maximum limits. The *wrist drop* on my right side, which Alistair Macafee had described to the junior doctors, was caused by paralysis of the nerve; Radial Nerve Palsy. By then, six months after the crash, it caused burning nerve pain to throb and sear through my arm.

My hand could not stay upright without support. I could hold the palm facing upwards, supination, but when I turned it over to a downwards position, pronation, it flopped forward limply.

It was therefore a huge moment when, without any previous indication of improvement, a straight wrist interrupted my pre-bed routine and I jumped around my Church Hill bedroom like a lottery winner.

Earlier that month, an ENT consultant at Belfast's City Hospital had repaired the hole in my left eardrum. The operation required the grafting of tissue from under the hairline above the ear and was a success, tinnitus notwithstanding. The following day I watched the Grand National on the hospital ward.

There had been many fences to jump in my endurance test, but at least I was still in the race. I had been through it all with doctors, physiotherapists, psychotherapists, occupational therapists, speech therapists and clinical psychologists. It had been a mental and physical marathon—my own Grand National, but I was winning.

With my hand and ear fixed, and with every other part of my repaired body in some form of working order, I determined that it was time to get on. I knew that nothing short of the total return of my former mental capacity would suffice in the demanding financial markets in which I hoped to succeed. I needed to go back to work.

On Friday, April 28, 1989, six and a half months after the accident, I left the Joss Cardwell Rehabilitation Unit for the last time. At the time of my initial consultation, the in-house doctor had advised that I might spend a year there. After four months of daily, intensive therapy, I was on my way.

Two days later, Paddy dropped my holdall bag and me at the pick-up point outside Omagh Library, where I waited for a private coach that carried young people to Dublin from Donegal and Tyrone. There was no fuss, no leaving party, nobody but a few unknown students, waiting to return to college, and me.

I was still twenty-five percent, or three stone, lighter, having added little weight since the low point when the wires were prised from my jaw, and did not look out of place among my more youthful travelling companions.

It was like it had been five and a half years before, when I had made my way from the nearby bus depot to the student halls at Queen's University in Belfast; and, like then, I did not know what the future held.

More than eighteen months earlier, I had arrived in Dublin at the right time—at the beginning of a massive growth phase for the investment industry. I was part of a new breed of bank-employed financial analysts who advised asset managers on what shares to buy or sell, and soon found myself responsible for million-dollar investment decisions.

I had learned that it was important to make the research reports interesting, to capture the attention of the investment manager who was usually swamped by a constant flow of information.

In a note extolling the virtues of the UK condom manufacturer, LIG Plc., I had recommended buying the shares because of the *penetration* of their leading brand, Durex, the *thrust* of the business, and the high level of *satisfaction* achieved.

That hand-written note had caused much merriment in the executive assistant pool, one of whom was charged with putting it into print.

As UIB sought to widen its holdings of shares internationally, the colleague who had fainted at the hospital and I had been given the task of cutting the number of holdings in the Irish Equity portfolio from forty to twenty. That required us to be ruthless. Often, we would meet with a company's executives in the morning and begin selling our entire shareholding in the afternoon.

My ability to make fast decisions meant that my star rose quickly and within six months of joining the bank, I had been appointed head of a newly-formed, three-person, research unit, and given a 50% pay rise.

Less than eight years after I swapped manual labour on the shop floor of the kitchen factory for Omagh Tech, I was shooting through the ranks at UIB.

There had been no plan and many missteps, but I was on course to graduate from the research department and take my place among the elevated ranks of portfolio managers.

And then I crashed, thirteen months into that ascent.

Nearly seven-months after I last slept in Dublin, the suits that hung in my wardrobe were much too big for me. The weight loss was the only consequence of the accident that I was happy about.

I eyed a flash new Italian suit. The lightweight, light grey Zegna suit had a blue check and a purple silk lining. At five-foot-six, it was usual in my off-the-peg suit purchases that the pleated trouser legs had to be greatly shortened. That, added to the padded shoulders and double-breasted cut, made the suit look big, but smart.

Keen to avoid signs of weakness, I declined UIB Human Resources offer to work mornings-only for the first month, and on Tuesday, May 2, 1989, donned my smart new suit and caught a Dublin bus from Raheny to the city centre and retook my place in the fifty-screen dealing room at UIB's Headquarters, at Dublin's Ely Place.

My dealing room colleagues were also keen for me to settle slowly back into the pace of work, and it was several months before I re-emerged on the office social scene, which revolved around the local pub.

It was standing room only on most Thursday and Friday evenings, and at the best of times it was hard to hold a conversation. I was invariably half a foot smaller than my male colleagues, and, in order to be more easily understood, had to slow down my Northern Irish accent.

After a year of consuming no more than an alcohol-free lager, the consumption of even a pint of beer would make my spoken words slower still, until they descended into a slur and I struggled to be understood—something that caused panic in the faces of my work colleagues.

My brain was working perfectly well, but I could not always get the words out in sync with my thoughts. I still attended speech therapy lessons long after my return to work.

Moreover, beer, cold weather, or tiredness would result in a significant dragging of my left side. It was frustrating, but I recognised these problems and understood that, for the moment, I was not the man I was before.

I had been warned at rehab that the cerebral contusion could cause a 'cascading' of my emotions and identified with that. I might find a moderate joke hilariously funny or could be engulfed by grief at a mildly sad scene from an early-evening television soap. At times like these, I would talk with myself, scolding myself that the story wasn't funny or sad until the moment passed.

The monthly UIB policy meeting determined our ongoing investment strategy and was not a place for jokes or triviality. There, intelligent and experienced investment professionals sat for hours around a boardroom table discussing the outlook for global economies, currencies, and investment markets.

The value of billions of pounds of pension fund assets was at stake. Should we buy or sell. Should we invest our clients' money in global shares, bonds, property markets, or just hold cash?

The problem occurred when the Chairman used the word '*proactive*'—as he was wont to do. We needed to think ahead, be proactive and make our decisions before, not after, the global investment *crowd*. But for no reason other than his fondness of the word, I was overcome with amusement and had to bring on a self-induced bout of coughing to mask the laughter.

None of the dozen heads that looked my way were quite sure what to make of me as I left the room to compose myself. And as I learned later, at least half of the observers understandably thought; 'Shame—he's not the man he was before.'

CHAPTER SEVENTEEN

The Court Case

In February 1989, two months after the police visited me at Church Hill, an official letter arrived stating that 'due to lack of evidence' there would be no criminal action against either driver.

I now had every chance of winning in the civil courts.

'Oh no, not Martin *and* Christopher,' Jim Montague – Mum's solicitor and executor, and an advisor to me during my early years running the pub – had said, in reaction to news of my reported death, one year after Martin's.

With a civil court action to pursue, Jim was soon firmly back in my life, adding purpose to my legal claim.

An engineer's report was commissioned to examine the final resting positions of both vehicles, their relative weights, likely speeds at the time of impact, marks on the road, and damage caused by the lorry to Mr. Cosgrove's garden wall.

Both vehicles had come to rest on my side of the road and the report suggested that, on balance, it was likely the lorry had struck the garden wall and run over me while my car was on the correct side of the road.

We also commissioned a report by a Belfast-based forensic scientist, and I was back at work in Dublin when Jim called with news.

'Are you sitting down Christopher?' he said. He had given

me constant free advice nearly ten years before, and I knew that he was not in any way prone to hyperbole. 'I have in front of me the forensic report that we have been waiting on, and it could not be clearer. Let me read it to you; "I have examined the direction and trajectory of the impact to the driver's side of the damaged Renault 5 car and conclude that the accident could only have been caused by the lorry crossing the road and hitting the car, and not the other way around."'

Halleluiah. It was time to go to court.

'We will lodge a petition against Aidan Devlin and Hoey Transport with the High Court in Belfast,' he concluded.

But when Jim wrote to Hoey Transport seeking details of their legal representation, he learned that they had lodged a separate and prior petition against me in the Irish Republic. Recent changes to EU law allowed a civil action to be heard in either party's jurisdiction, rather than in the actual country of the accident.

It was to be a case of claim and counterclaim, to be heard south of the border by a single judge and no jury. I was at a big disadvantage. I was to be the defendant at Dundalk Circuit Court, and worse still, I was about to lose the main plank of evidence supporting my case.

Just months before, the IRA had ambushed and murdered two RUC officers, Chief Superintendent Harry Breen and Superintendent Bob Buchanan, as they returned from a meeting with Garda, at Dundalk Police Station. That happened at Jonesborough, South Armagh, a few miles from where my crash took place and would many years later be the focus of Ireland's Smithwick Tribunal that investigated collusion between Dundalk Garda and the IRA.

'I'm sorry to say Christopher, but our forensic scientist has worked with the RUC, and I doubt very much that he will cross the border to give evidence,' concluded my legal advisor.

The car had been crushed at the breaker's yard and no other forensic analysis was possible.

I now needed new legal representation and appointed UIB's advisors, Arthur Cox & Co of St Stephen's Green, Dublin. They were ultimately employed by my insurance company to defend the Hoey Transport Ltd. claim against me but were not mandated to prosecute on my behalf.

Without the forensic scientist, the principal focus of the defence relied on the evidence of the engineer, which was supportive to my case, but not conclusive.

A senior work colleague, Harry White, who had passed the scene within fifteen minutes of the accident, but did not recognise my car, would be able to give evidence regarding the spread of debris on my side of the road, corroborating the engineer's evidence. So too would Fergus Cosgrove. But neither had witnessed the crash.

I had, therefore, some technical evidence and no memory of what had happened. But that would not stop me pressing my legal advisors to bring a prosecution against the absent lorry driver, Aidan Devlin.

Two more years would pass before we were ready to go to court. Harry, who had conducted the interview process that led to me being hired by UIB, was a man that I trusted and admired. I had been promoted to work with him as an assistant portfolio manager and was once again on top of my investment game.

In the weeks before the Civil Court case in early 1991, he invited me to join a lunch in Dublin with Paul Roy, a senior City figure, and soon-to-be CEO of Smith New Court Plc. (SNC).

Then, earning twenty thousand pounds a year, high personal taxation and a room rented in a new house, meant that there was little left at the end of every month. And with the cost of prosecuting the Civil Court action falling to me, I was facing a financial crisis should I lose.

I thought little of that when I went to lunch at Dublin's best restaurant, run by the legendary chef Patrick Guilbaud, and listened as our City guest told us about his business, the deals he had done, was doing, and hoped to do. The numbers got bigger and bigger as the conversation wore on: one hundred million here, five hundred million there, and a billion to complete the circle.

It was the first time I had been face-to-face with a real City player—with a man who would later succeed at the upper reaches of the American investment bank, Merrill Lynch & Co Inc.

SNC had not been a success in Ireland, and Paul had come to Dublin to pick the brains of his old friend, Harry. I had joined the lunch thanks to Harry's goodwill, but was quick to decide on a solution to Paul's problem.

An opportunity to present my case arose on the next working day, when Paul telephoned to offer us the opportunity to participate in a four-hundred-million-pound offering that SNC was handling on behalf of Hanson Plc.

We had read about the deal on the newswires prior to his call and knew that it suited our portfolio to participate.

As an SNC Executive Director, it was not normally his remit to make calls on daily business deals, but he did so that day as a matter of goodwill to his lunch partners.

'I'd like to take a million pounds' worth,' I replied, once he finished outlining the offer, a figure that took him by surprise. It was the opportunity I needed to impress.

Later that day, I called him in London and suggested he needed an Irishman to boost his business with Irish institutions.

'Yes,' he said, 'but who?'

'Me,' I replied.

'You Irish, you have a nerve!' laughed Paul. 'Okay, can you come to London for an interview with my stockbroking colleagues?'

I was delighted with the response but, having already run the idea past Harry, who supported my plans, felt it appropriate to add the caveat that I would only take the job if I were to lose the pending court action.

Four days later, I saw the mirrored reflection of my two-year-old Zegna suit as I entered the lift to depart SNC's London headquarters. I had grown into it and kept it aside for my most important meetings.

'How do you think it went?' I asked, as Paul Roy followed me into the lift.

'It went fine,' said Paul, who had joined the latter part of my interview with his Head of Sales. 'I need to talk with my colleague, but yes, you'll be a great addition to the team.'

'But I'm not totally sure that I'll come,' I replied. 'The court case is next month.'

'Look, join us in any event. You'll love it here,' he said, firmly. 'We'll provide you with a nice apartment for a month or two until you can sort yourself out. And we'll take up an offer of some expensive corporate hospitality at the Walker Cup at Portmarnock in July, so that we can launch you as our new man in Ireland. Phil Mickelson will be playing for the USA—it'll be huge.'

He had it all worked out and his enthusiasm swayed me. My ultimate boss at UIB was the Club Captain at Dublin's Portmarnock Golf Club, so I had heard lots about Phil Mickelson and the Walker Cup, and I liked the idea of being SNC's 'new man in Ireland'.

'Okay, yes. I'll come, no matter what!' I said, as we shook hands in the foyer.

'Fantastic, we'll get a contract out to you on Monday. And we'll buy you a new suit!' he said flipping my ample lapel.

We smiled and went our separate ways.

A month later SNC made international headlines by providing corporate raider Hanson Plc with a strategic 2.8% stake in the £8.5bn/$15bn, ICI Plc., the UK's third-largest company.

It was a huge risk, going 'naked-short' 20 million shares at £12 per share (£240m); that is, they sold shares they didn't actually own and would now rely on their City stockbroking franchise to acquire the stock and avoid making a loss.

The gambit paid off but the risk was such that Lord Hanson, who had already made $15bn of asset-stripping acquisitions globally, reportedly uttered the following words to Paul and his colleague Michael Marks in an SNC elevator: 'You guys have big balls!'

Throughout my life I had sought out significant males, some of whom were uncles.

People like Brother O'Reilly, Donal Donnelly, Jim Montague, Youth Leaders at Omagh Boys & Girls Club, tutors at Omagh Tech and Queen's, Harry White, my wonderful surgeon, Alistair Macafee, and now Paul Roy, and later Dan Tully, cared.

In Mr. Diarmuid O'Donovan, the Senior Counsel (SC), and later High Court Judge, appointed by Arthur Cox & Co. to consider my prosecution of the transport company, I was to find another.

At our first meeting he made it clear that my case had to stand on its own merits, or he would not prosecute. Despite that risk, and an understanding that barristers do not take on cases they do not expect to win, I could not have been happier that he was on my side.

'It's going to be very difficult to win this case,' my SC advised again on the journey from Dublin to Fergus's South Armagh home. 'You not being able to remember what happened makes it very difficult, especially if the lorry driver proves to be a reliable witness. While we have the engineer's evidence supporting your case, no doubt they will have something similar,' he added, forlornly.

'But what about the forensic report?' I said. 'Surely the judge must take that into account?'

'He will read the report, but he will not be able to admit it to evidence, nor use it in deciding on the verdict, unless you can convince the forensic expert to cross the border.'

Settling the initial claim on behalf of The Prudential Insurance Company, with whom I had third-party legal cover, was the easy option for him. The risk for me was that I would be liable to settle Mr. O'Donovan's fee for my counterclaim, should I lose.

'Look, the passenger side of the lorry clipped that coping stone,' said Fergus, pointing to the end of his garden wall where the road's hard shoulder had narrowed from about one-and-a-half-metres to only half-a-metre. 'He may well have been mooching for cigarettes or checking his tachograph and hadn't noticed the narrowing of the verge,' Fergus added passionately. 'And look, he finished up in that field over there on Chris's side of the road and took a straight-line route to get there. And Chris's car was down there on his own hard shoulder.'

'Okay, okay, we'll give it a go; we'll go to court,' said my legal talisman.

Hearts and minds had worked their wonder, but I couldn't help thinking that Mr. O'Donovan was doing it against his better judgement; doing it because he felt sorry for me.

Jesus, I thought, *what will happen if I lose? At twenty-eight years old, I'll be broke.*

'We have asked for one hundred and eighty-five thousand pounds in compensation,' said Mr. O'Donovan one day later, in April 1991, 'and we'll be negotiating with the other side's legal representative's right up until we're due in court. We're third on the list,' he said. 'My guess is that we'll probably have to come back tomorrow. But don't go anywhere in case we're called,' he finished, before rushing off to talk with the insurance company's legal counsel.

In the hours that followed, Fergus and I kicked our heels in the dull hallway of the decrepit Dundalk Court House. Rising damp grew up its grey walls and paint flaked off its ceiling. The red-and-black tiled floor on which we stood was gently curved in parts by the wear and tear of a hundred years of footsteps.

All the time I could see another group of three people, two men and a woman, moving from place to place around the same limited confines.

'If that's them,' I said to Fergus, 'which one's the driver?'

'The tall one,' he said guessing. 'The other two are probably the owners.'

'They've made an offer,' said my barrister to break the silence that followed, leaning between Fergus and me to quietly impart the news.

'What is it?' I asked.

'£45,000,' he whispered, 'but I believe we can get double that.'

'No, I'm sorry,' I said right away. 'I want to go to court; I want to see the whites of the lorry driver's eyes. I want to know what happened.'

'And if I can make it £90,000?' he replied.

The idea of a settlement had not occurred to me. I had come to court that day prepared for battle, and my response to the proposition was swift.

'No, I'm sorry,' I repeated, 'I want to go to court.' It was to be cathartic.

It was a Thursday morning when Fergus and I waited in

the hallway of Dundalk Court House with my solicitor, his assistant and the senior and junior counsel, James Nugent (SC) and Patrick Gallagher, defending me on behalf of my insurance company.

Diarmuid O'Donovan stood nearby with the other side's legal representatives.

Earlier I had watched from the public gallery, waiting for an end to a medical negligence claim against a GP, praying for a speedy end to the case. My legal team's view was that the presiding judge would be the more sympathetic of the two judges at the Circuit Court. If the medical negligence case ended in good time, we hoped he would proceed straight to my case, but it was not to be.

As we instead waited to face Judge Johnston, the other parties to the case stood nearby waiting, like us, for an end to the discussion between our barristers. I wondered again which of them was the absent driver.

For most of the next two days in the case of Hoey Transport v Christopher McGale, I sat in the elevated public gallery staring straight across the courtroom at my opponents.

The narrow confines of courtroom benches were not designed for tall men like Aidan Devlin, and he was forced to constantly adjust his seating position by leaning his head across the benches in front of him or sitting sideways and crossing his legs.

I focused on him often in that seat, hoping to make eye contact, but never did.

We watched the legal teams and the judge in the pit below as the technical experts that had been assembled by both sides gave their evidence. And as Mr. O'Donovan had suggested, there was strong conviction on both sides that the other party was responsible.

Tension in the courtroom was high as Diarmuid O'Donovan harangued Aidan Devlin in a masterful display of cross-examination:

'Were you tired that morning?

'Were you smoking?'

'Were you reaching for papers?'

'Were you speeding?'

'Were you affected by the road conditions?'

'Was visibility poor?'

'Did you see a car coming towards you?'

'No,' was the answer to every question, except the last two.

'Visibility was poor. But I could see two sets of car headlights coming towards me. One was in the middle of the road, probably trying to overtake the other. I pulled onto the hard shoulder to avoid the oncoming car, but it kept coming at me. I clipped the pillar at the end of the garden wall and shot across the road. I couldn't avoid him; it wasn't my fault.'

For the first time since my early days in hospital, seeds of doubt were planted in my mind. He still did not look at me and did not offer any sign of condolence, but I could not be sure that he was lying.

Jesus, maybe I had caused the crash after all.

The lorry driver's reference to two cars coming towards him led to him being followed into the witness box by another witness for the prosecution—the driver of the other car.

That chap said that he had pulled out of a side road and was heading southwards down the hill towards Dundalk. No car was on the northern horizon when he pulled onto the main road, but as he drove onwards at a slow speed in poor light conditions, he became aware of a car closing on him from behind—my car.

He had passed the lorry before the collision happened and did not see the impact but became aware of the crash when he heard the bang. He could not say if I was exceeding the national speed limit, as he was driving slowly.

Fergus and Harry attended but were not called to give

evidence about the spread of debris on my side of the road and the two engineers acting for both parties presented evidence. All that was left was for me to take my place in the dock the next morning.

'Will Mr. McGale be taking the witness stand?' asked Judge Johnston.

'Yes, he is keen to do that,' replied my counsel.

I was the last witness and was ready for the challenge. Nearly two and a half years had passed since Fergus had spoken those immortal words; 'There is no way that you caused that crash,' and I was keen to help prove that.

I had been emotionally drained waiting for that day, that moment. But in truth, I had nothing to add, no new evidence to enlist, and like a Christian Martyr on a cross, I had taken the stand to show I 'believed'.

Maybe if they see how much I have suffered they will tell the truth, tell the judge what really happened, I pondered, *maybe the horror of being in the dock will prompt some memories, maybe I just want to see the reaction of my enemies.*

And so, I made my way to the witness stand in front of the judge, and for the first time made clear eye contact with the lorry driver.

I felt only a little nervous as I went down the steps of the courtroom to the witness box. But, when I put my hand on the bible and promised to tell the truth, the whole truth, and nothing but the truth, I felt a surge.

My lawyer questioned in sympathetic tones, knowing I had no evidence to offer.

'Were you the person driving the Renault car, registration CUI 697, that was involved in the collision on the A1 Belfast to Dublin Road on October 13, 1988?'

'Yes, I was.'

'What do you remember about the crash?'

'Nothing at all.'

'When did you become aware of the accident?'

'When I woke up in hospital.'

As those words came out, I slumped forward, laid my head in my hands and cried and cried.

'We'll take a break while Mr. McGale composes himself,' said Judge Johnston.

I was provided with a glass of water and made my way to the corridor outside, before returning to the dock fifteen minutes later. On resumption, my lawyer said that he had no more questions, and the lawyer for the other side echoed that.

Then Mr. O'Donovan handed the judge a clear plastic folder that I had given to him a few days before.

It contained what I euphemistically called my 'holiday snaps', close-up images of my injuries taken before and after the five surgeon, five-hour operation, to put me back together again.

Nothing was said as he reviewed the images, which I knew intimately. I saw the open hole in my right elbow, the elbow no longer there; and the hole in my left hand, where three of the five metacarpals had been severed, their sprung sinews protruding from the bloodied valley in my hand like strings from a thrashed guitar.

The photographs were taken by a hospital-appointed photographer and passed to me for the court case by the maxillofacial surgeon, Mr. Ramsey-Baggs.

I had always thought that a string of red tape, which could be seen in two pre-operation pictures, was somehow holding my face together. It ran below my nose and was tied across and behind my ears, above my broken jaw.

Above and below were crevice-like facial lacerations, which would be expertly repaired by Mr. Ramsey-Baggs.

In response to my question about the function of the red tape, he replied, 'The tape is white—it only looks red because it's soaked in blood. It is used to tie the nasotracheal tube (i.e.

the one down into the top part of your lungs to allow you to be anaesthetised). The tape is in position to stop it falling (or being pulled) out. Look carefully and you will see that it is tied around the tube just below your nose. It's not a swab tie. The tube coming out of your mouth is into your stomach. It's to prevent a build-up of acid and swallowed blood.'

A post-op picture showed both tubes inserted in my nostrils, which the judge saw as he carefully examined each image. He asked me to come to his chambers along with my lawyer and beckoned me to strip to the waist to exhibit my injuries. I had completely recovered my poise and hoped to impress on him the extent of the damage done to me.

After I undressed, I showed the judge that with only thirty degrees of movement in the bent right arm, it was necessary to first put that arm into my shirt's sleeve, as it is impossible to dress otherwise.

I showed him how my arms could not extend to reach into an overhead locker, like that of an aircraft, and how the right arm moved only with gravity once it got below a ninety-degree angle.

I showed him how my two hands moved at different speeds when being opened and closed, and the hypertension in my left foot that I could set into perpetual motion by placing the ball of my foot on the floor and raising the heel as I sat.

Pointing to the ragged scars on my left hand and right elbow, I told him about the nightmare I had suffered in the months after the accident, the dream about my arms and hands being mutilated by four large dogs and how they tore me apart as I tried to pull away.

He said that he would take the weekend to consider the evidence and would give his verdict on Monday morning. I left the chamber with more hope than I had entered it with.

While I waited for the verdict, and during the trial itself, I dreamed constantly of courtroom scenes, my mind replaying events as if I were directing the cast in a movie production.

Those dreams did not, however, break open the dark room in my brain where the memories of my head-on collision with the twenty-tonne lorry had been sealed. At that moment, those insights remained deeply buried in my brain—only to be revealed on the Aer Lingus flight to London, twenty-two years later.

It was Tuesday morning when the Judge finally revealed the outcome of his deliberations, having told us on the Monday morning that he had not yet decided on a verdict. The delay gave me more of a chance, I reasoned; maybe it was just impossible to decide who was to blame. Maybe he'd instruct both insurance companies to pay compensation.

I sat with my constant companion, Fergus, as Judge Johnston explained the basis of his verdict and quickly gathered the significance. As his summation continued, the certainty of the verdict became more apparent.

I sat back on the wooden bench in the public gallery and was overcome by a sense of mirth, such that I almost laughed. Gallows humour had engulfed me. I was going to lose.

The judge could not accept as admissible the in-camera evidence from the forensic scientist. He had two sets of conflicting engineers' evidence. None of the witnesses for either side had seen the collision, and as no one except the two drivers themselves could shed light on what had happened, he only had the evidence of the lorry driver.

Since he had 'no reason to disbelieve Mr. Devlin', he had no choice but to find in favour of the claimant, Hoey Transport Ltd.

The judge didn't look my way after delivering the verdict.

In the gallery opposite, I watched Aidan Devlin and the Hoeys embrace and backslap one another. They were jumping with joy, despite the fact that this was a Civil Court matter and we were claiming off each other's insurance companies.

But it wasn't about money for me, and I continued to feel perversely happy. It had been a worthwhile exercise, an exorcism.

The euphoria across the courtroom made me smile even more, and I sat back as a broad grin unfolded. I watched to see if they would look my way, maybe even remonstrate with me, but they never did.

My legal representatives, two senior counsel, one junior, and my solicitor, had formed a huddle with Mr. O'Donovan's arms flailing in the narrow space.

'I'm sorry, Chris,' said Mr. O'Donovan, when I made my way down to the legal pit.

'We gave it our best shot,' I said. 'You couldn't have done more. Thank you for taking the case and working so hard on my behalf.'

'We'll appeal,' he said, but was quickly corrected by his SC colleague.

'We can't appeal,' said that sage, 'unless we have new evidence.'

'What about the forensic guy, can you talk with him?' said Mr. O'Donovan with a final burst.

'No,' I said, 'he'll never come here. It's over. We have nothing more to offer. Thank you all for working so hard on my behalf. It is not the end of the world—nobody died…'

There would be no appeal.

The fight was over.

I had seen the whites of the lorry driver's eyes, and, having done so, was no longer certain that I was an innocent victim.

When at last I received written confirmation from Arthur Cox & Co, confirming that my barristers had concluded that there was no basis for appeal, I read aloud the words that followed: 'However, Mr. Diarmuid O'Donovan was humbled by your response to the verdict, and has decided to waive his fees. As such your account with Arthur Cox & Co is now clear. We therefore wish to thank you for bringing your case to us and offer our very best wishes with your future endeavours. Yours etc. David Piggott.'

Eleven months after the court case, on March 26, 1992, WPC Colleen McMurray was travelling in an unmarked patrol car on Newry's Merchants Quay, when she was struck by a horizontal Mark 12 mortar, launched remotely by the IRA.

The atrocity took place at half-past eleven pm and Colleen died hours later at the at Daisy Hill Hospital, the place where they had saved my life. A male colleague lost both legs in the attack.

She was thirty-four years old and had been married for only eighteen months.

Cardinal Cahal Daly described Constable McMurray's killing as 'brutal and despicable', and said, 'she was herself greatly respected as a caring young woman who saw her policing work as a service to all sections of the community.'

The coroner said, 'A young woman from the island of Ireland with the name of Colleen represents an ideal of Irish nationality worldwide. Colleen McMurray was brutally murdered by men who claim to be in pursuit of such an ideal.'

A newspaper memorial notice I read many years later said appropriately, that she was 'resting where no shadows fall.'

PART FOUR

The City

CHAPTER EIGHTEEN

Warzone

'Do you know you're going to a warzone?' asked the reporter from Dublin's Evening Herald newspaper, as a camera flashed in my face. It was 5am in late June 1991 and I was standing in a queue at Dublin Airport with nuns on their way to Medjugorje.

We were waiting to board a much-delayed charter-flight to Croatia, a country that had in the days before declared its independence from the splintering Yugoslavia.

'I'm from Tyrone, we're used to these things.'

The newspaper reported my weary reply the following day, along with a passport-sized picture of me at the airport.

It was the cause of merriment for my Dublin friends, whom I met in the days that followed—the flight to Split having been cancelled.

After concluding my notice period at UIB, I had planned a weeklong break in Dubrovnik before the move to London.

I had bought a copy of James Joyce's *Ulysses* at Dublin Airport, but as Joyce may have said, it was a 'highfalutin' idea that I could ever navigate my way from the beginning to the end of his 'stream of consciousness' tome.

It was a book for my brother Paul, not me, and never got read, but acted as a pillow while I wiled away the hours awaiting the flight that was not to be.

It was hot when I landed at Heathrow Airport at 8am on

July 15, 1991, two and a half months after the court case.

I balked at the price estimated by a London black cab driver to take me to an address near Latimer Road underground station, where I would attend lectures in the week ahead. That would prepare me for a regulatory exam to become a regulated stockbroker at Paul Roy's SNC.

All my worldly possessions were packed into two wheel-less suitcases and two holdall bags that crisscrossed my neck like the gun-belt of a wild-west gunslinger. I was already running late when I took the down-escalator to Heathrow's Terminal 1 tube station.

The heat, weight of the bags, my crocked arms and creaking spine meant that I had to set down every few steps. Sweat seeped from every pore as I followed the long underground walkway towards the trains.

There was standing room only when I stepped on to the Piccadilly Line train headed for Kings Cross station, where I would endure a Grand National-like journey up and down stairwells and escalators.

Having arrived on the day of my lectures, I had to make my way directly to the training centre and I was bushed and flushed by Latimer Road one and a half hours later. I was dressed in a jacket, trousers, and flat shoes, inappropriate for the hot and mountainous trek I had endured.

Sweat streamed down my face as I heaved my baggage one more time out of the underground station and dropped everything in a heap at the feet of a road sweeper who was tending the steps of the station.

My jacket, now wedged in an armpit, was flung on top of the baggage pile, and my slim-fitting shirt clung to me like a model in a wet tee-shirt competition.

'A tough journey?' said the litter man with a strong Irish brogue.

'Yes. Bloody awful. Jesus, I'm sore,' I said, raising my arms to Heaven and crushing together my shoulder blades.

'Are you from the North?'

'Yes, from Tyrone. And you?'

'Westmeath.'

'I read an article on the aeroplane about your hurling team; losing good players due to emigration,' I said, one Irish emigrant to another.

'Every time we get a team together, we lose them, as the men go overseas for work. Are you looking for work?' he asked.

'No, I'm attending a study course near here, and I'm already an hour late. Can I get a black cab here?' I asked, observing the quiet streets.

'No, you'd be lucky to find one here. Where're you going?'

'The Financial Training Centre. Is it nearby?'

'It's about half a mile away,' he said.

I groaned at the prospect of another bout of hauling my bags in the sweltering heat.

'I'll tell you what—put your bags onto my trolley and I'll take you there.'

I didn't hesitate, and my new-found Irish buddy from Mullingar loaded my bags onto his cart and ferried them down the road.

I told him about the career I hoped to have in The City, and how I had started as a bookie's runner in Omagh.

'I have seen *Wall Street*, the movie, but never met a stockbroker,' said my chariot driver, 'and I never thought for a minute that you might be one.'

'Nor did I my friend, nor did I. With my whole world being ferried on your dustcart, I feel more like Mick Dundee than Gordon Gekko! I don't know how I got here.' We both laughed heartily.

We were approaching the steel and glass structure of the financial training building, where it was possible to see out but not in. Inside looking out as the road sweeper and the stockbroker approached, were soon-to-be SNC colleagues.

One week later, when I arrived fully regulated and ready for work at my new City office, news of my trash-car joyride was there to greet me.

Mick Dundee continued to follow me around in my early days exploring London.

SNC had provided me with a month-long lease of a fantastic one-bed apartment in New Cavendish Street, and I spent most evenings wandering around the West End, establishing my bearings in the Theatreland areas of Piccadilly, Shaftsbury Avenue, Leicester Square, Covent Garden and The Strand.

One evening I exited my apartment block via an alternative elevator shaft to see where it might take me. It was a lift to the car park, but when the door opened, the dimly lit hallway was illuminated only by the outline of a towering African woman in a flowery dress and headdress. Her unexpected appearance made me gasp and nearly jump.

'I'm sorry,' I said, as she gave me a withering look and I rushed past into the car park.

In joining SNC my annual salary had doubled, and with lower taxation and currency gains, my net pay trebled. But having lost the legal action, I was overdrawn and broke.

After a month in New Cavendish Street, I found digs in Hammersmith with a delightfully posh widow called Mrs. Gent. She had an ancient, obese, Siamese cat called Desmond, an animal that moved around the house like a slumbering pig and shed black and white hairs on the red velvet settee and carpeted living room.

For £100 per week I had a bedroom and bathroom in the attic space and had allocated space in the fridge-freezer.

'I now have three lovely boys living with me,' said Mrs. Gent soon after I moved in. That included a long-term resident she called big Chris, little Chris (me), and Desmond, who at 16 human years was, like his owner, an octogenarian in cat years. But like Mick Dundee, The Troubles followed me, and less than two weeks after I moved in, three IRA incendiary devices were discovered under a seat at the nearby Hammersmith Underground depot.

Mrs. Gent called my employer and rent guarantor, Paul Roy.

'Mr. Roy,' she said in strong, elaborated, tones to my boss, who on a daily basis was responsible for hundreds of millions of pounds' worth of client business, 'I have someone here who lives in my attic, Chris McGale. He says he works for you.'

'I am glad to have cleared that up,' Mrs. Gent said cheerily to me later, but she didn't tell me what she'd said to Paul after he'd clarified my position: 'Oh good, I thought he might be in the IRA!'

I had begun my investment career in Dublin at the time of the stock market crash of 1987 and moved to London towards the end of the subsequent four-year down-cycle. My timing could not have been better.

Rising stock market indices, at fixed commission rates, in each of the ten succeeding years, meant rising revenues for the firm and rising pay for me.

But 1992 started badly for SNC as one of our corporate clients attracted lots of negative press for us. We were the Stock Exchange sponsor of Amber Day Plc., which had seen its share price collapse and its Chief Executive resign.

'Philip Green will never work in The City again,' declared an Executive Director to a packed room of salespeople, sales traders, and market makers.

SNC market makers were prepared to take bigger risks. Our trading floor had a team of one hundred men, and our dealers had a deserved reputation of being the biggest and best of The City traders. That was important if my clients wanted to place multi-million-pound orders to buy or sell stocks.

I had joined an expanding team of mostly male stockbrokers. In City jargon, my job was to *smile and dial*. We smiled, we dialled, and hoped that each telephone call would result in a revenue generating client order. For a master salesman like me, it felt like all I had to do to succeed was turn up for work.

I knew hardly anyone in London and adopted a 'live-to-work' mantra. I returned to Hammersmith only to dine at local restaurants and sleep.

I worked late most evenings, reading investment notes produced behind imaginary 'Chinese Walls' by the adjacent SNC research department.

As making money was the thing that most excited me, I would often have a Halleluiah moment and finish a long day buzzing about how I might sell a great research idea to clients the following morning.

Being alone on the trading floor gave me opportunities to meet and chat with SNC executives as they left their so-called 'goldfish bowl' glass offices that surrounded the dealing room.

On one such evening I was introduced to Cyril Stein, Chairman, Ladbrokes Plc, SNC's largest corporate client, and a hero of mine. In on-track *tic-tac*, a fascinating system of hand-signalling used by racecourse bookmakers when deploying funds to shorten starting prices, Ladbrokes was identified by the *Magic Sign*, a hand movement like drawing a circle over the head.

Under Cyril's leadership, Ladbrokes had become the UK's largest bookmaker with nearly 2000 offices and a 25% share of the £5bn market, and such was my enthusiasm that he agreed to travel with me to Dublin for prospective investor meetings.

After an early-morning business-class flight, it was clear Cyril was not looking forward to the day ahead, even though I had arranged a benign schedule of four one-to-one institutional meetings.

He was not a natural raconteur, and at our final, post-lunch, meeting the question and answer session started slowly.

Much to Cyril's chagrin, the portfolio manager knew virtually nothing about Ladbrokes or horseracing and read from a prepared list of questions as he sought to build an understanding.

I found myself breaking the silences by answering questions, which appeared to suit Cyril. But as we approached the end of a seemingly eternal meeting, the prospective investor asked about bad debts.

'What do you mean?' said Cyril.

'I mean, what do you do when a punter doesn't pay his debts?'

'It doesn't happen,' Cyril mumbled after a pause.

'You mean everyone pays their gambling debts?'

'Yes,' said Cyril, firmly.

'It is honour amongst thieves,' I offered, seeking to break the impasse.

Cyril adopted a look of horror.

'That's not how I would describe it, there is trust on both sides,' he eventually followed, and pointed to his watch. We then shared a largely silent limo back to Dublin Airport, and no potential investors bought shares in Ladbrokes.

My efforts to bring UK corporates to Ireland were appreciated by Irish institutions and not long after I got my first large share trade from one of Dublin's most successful fund managers, whom I had known a little before moving to London.

He was a no-nonsense character who loved to trade in multi-million-pound deals, and I was in the right place to accommodate him.

When asked by a colleague why he sent so much business my way, he replied nonplussed, 'Sure, he's a friend of yours, isn't he?'

That apparently simple answer dovetailed with an equally simple mantra that pertained among the small group of 'big-hitting' brokers with whom I sat: the Irish for the Irish, the Scots for the Scots, the Jews for the Jews and the Old Etonians and other posh boys for each other. And it worked.

Although the SNC traders were predominantly Jewish, there were no religious trappings aside from the occasional skullcap or Kippah, and general observances of the Jewish New Year and Yom Kippur.

'You know you're joining a Jewish firm?' said a broker friend from Dublin on news that I was joining SNC. 'What's a Jewish firm?' I responded sincerely, having only ever encountered Catholics and Protestants.

I was six when The Troubles started and, having spent the next eighteen-years of my life as part of the tribal conflict, I had felt an unexpected emancipation when I arrived for work in Dublin.

Amongst my friends and work colleagues, religion was never discussed, and talk of Northern Ireland was banned. The horrors of the conflict were an embarrassment to the southern-Irish educated classes.

In Omagh, almost everyone I knew thought of themselves as Irish, and most had Irish passports to prove it. And by the early 1990s, Gaelic Football teams from Ulster were once-again winning the thirty-two county All Ireland Championship – if not my beloved Tyrone. But the ongoing war meant that we northern Catholics mostly felt like second class citizens on both sides of the Irish border.

'We're Irish too,' I often thought, but seldom said in Dublin.

Twelve months into my new life in London, in July 1992, I caught the bottom of a three-year housing market crash and purchased a three-bed refurbished flat in Hammersmith for £125,000. It was funded by a 100% mortgage secured on my rapidly growing salary.

I continued to travel back and forth to Omagh – as Paddy was dying.

A photograph of Paddy and I stood on a sideboard in London. It was taken at the now-tenanted Kate's Bar on March 22, 1992. It showed family and friends celebrating his 70th birthday. He never let us forget that date—two, two, three, two, two (22/03/1922).

Having 'taken on another man's family', we had not forgotten what he had done for us. As the family, nieces, nephews, and grandchildren queued to be photographed, while showering him with hugs and kisses, he pointed proudly to a badge fixed to the lapel of his jacket. It read: 'I'm only 70!' He had one more year to live.

Paul was the final McGale to arrive at Paddy's hospital bedside just before he died. He had a dilated aneurism and hung on to life until Paul's arrival from Scotland.

Five years before, Paul had visited me and Paddy at Church Hill at Christmas 1988, two months after my crash.

'The Christian Brothers didn't do me any harm,' I'd said then, without much thought, as we sat in front of a blazing Church Hill fire, having always looked back fondly at my time with Brother O'Reilly. To my mind, we were just another troubled family growing up in The Troubles.

'That's because you were never punched unconscious in a tiny school office,' raged my brother as he leapt to his feet, his face puce with anger.

He was then a storeman and was studying Chemistry at the Open University. He would later teach the subject.

Paddy's funeral lunch was celebratory, with all the male mourners obliged to drink nothing but his favourite tipple, Powers Whiskey mixed with water, such that each round of drinks amounted to twenty or more.

Paul had now been sober for six years and took no part in

the drinking game.

Twelve months before, while holidaying in the west of Ireland with a girlfriend, to our great surprise Paul and his wife Jane came around a corner and bumped into us on Main Street, Dingle, Co. Kerry. We had travelled from London and they from Edinburgh and agreed to meet for dinner. He drank water, I drank wine.

It was the story of our lives: he drank coffee, I drank tea. He read books, I read newspapers.

We argued the night before the funeral, debating the route of the pallbearers from the Church Hill townhouse to the nearby Sacred Heart Church. Was it to be straight up the hill, or, like Martin's, around the block, past Kate's Bar? I wanted the latter.

As children we fought over Sunday-chicken wishbones. We fought as teenagers, we fought in hospital, we fought when he was drunk, we fought when he was sober. Nothing had changed, except that punches were no longer being thrown.

With Paul and Jane at Dingle, Co Kerry, 1992

CHAPTER NINETEEN

Wall Street: The Gamble

'We're earning more than *The Arsenal*,' laughed Desmond, my only gambling confidant at SNC, as bonus time approached.

It was the end of April 1993 and I was nearly two years into my City career. First Division professional footballers then earned around £200,000. I knew I could make even more money away from SNC but had no plan to do so.

On my return from Paddy's funeral, I was beckoned into one of the goldfish bowl offices by the Head of Trading who commiserated with me and told me that his mother had just died. I was happy to be part of the SNC family.

My job was to disseminate the firm's research ideas, both Buy and Sell, seeking to generate buying and selling order flow for my trading colleagues and cash commissions for me.

SNC charged a commission rate of 0.2% of the value of every buy or sell trade placed; that is, £2,000 from every £1 million client order was added to the revenue line of my personal profit and loss account, from which my bonus would be paid at the year-end.

By now I was so busy with client business that I liked to misquote Linda Evangelista: *I wouldn't pick up the phone for less than £1m.*

'Where are you going?' said a trader colleague from his

swivel chair as I passed to exit the dealing room during a mid-morning lull.

'Goldman Sachs,' I replied spontaneously, whereas I was in fact going to a next-door sandwich bar.

'Chris, could you come to my office?' came the phone call to my desk as soon as I returned.

'What's this about Goldman?' asked Paul Roy as I entered his office.

'Goldman?' When the penny dropped, I laughed out loud. 'Nah, that was just something I said as I passed the market makers, there's nothing in that.'

'Look, your successes have not gone unnoticed, you're a very valuable member of the team. In fact, I had planned to raise your basic salary to £100,000 when bonuses are paid next week, and I want you to come along to our senior management offsite in June where we will discuss our plans for growing the business.'

The two-day offsite had been happening for a few years but was on a need-to-know basis; I had never heard of it.

My gambling was also on a need-to-know basis. I had for years conditioned myself to stay *schtum* and kept the highs and the lows to myself. Given the sums involved, to confide in an uninitiated friend or colleague was to invite incredulity.

In the week before the SNC offsite, I was convinced that Tenby, trained by the champion trainer Henry Cecil, and the hot favourite for the 1993 Derby, would not win. By then I felt sufficiently empowered by my position as a *big swinging dick* broker to go public among my work colleagues.

I decided to become a bookie for the day and spread the word around the SNC dealing room that I would offer the Derby favourite at even-money (1/1) rather than the 4/5 offered by conventional bookies, and soon found a willing taker hoping to double his thousand-pound stake, rather than the £800 he would potentially win through the High-Street bookies.

By the time the Derby 'field' had passed Tattenham Corner with three of the twelve furlongs still to race, Tenby was among the leaders in second place, but I was counting the money. Twenty years of watching horse races on television and on the track told me that Tenby had no chance of winning. He finally crossed the finish line tenth out of the sixteen runners.

Bookies differed from SNC traders in that they offered only to sell—not buy or sell; that is, they were not a two-way 'exchange'. You could bet on, or buy, one or more horses in a race at the price offered, but you could never sell to a bookie.

You could not 'lay' Tenby as I had, unless you had a captive group of potentially interested punters, such as offering the Derby favourite at an attractive price to the SNC trading floor. My net of potential buyers was further widened through word of mouth. The punter who bet on Tenby was a City client of one of my broking colleagues.

With the ability to Buy and Sell a horse in a race, I had created the McGale Betting Exchange, just like SNC was part of the London Stock Exchange.

Years later, the biggest loss of my life was caused by an exchange, when I was invited to attend an early-stage investor meeting for a company that would revolutionise the UK betting market. They provided a platform through which gamblers could buy or sell, an exchange.

For whatever reason I did not attend. If I had, I would have met Ed Wray, a former JP Morgan & Co. banker, and his business partner, Andrew Black, a college dropout and professional gambler of my vintage.

Had I met them, I would have invested heavily in the company. In 2010 the company listed on the LSE with a value of £1.4 billion; Betfair. Even a 1% stake would have been worth £14m.

A year after laying Tenby to lose in the 1993 Derby, I got a taste for spread betting following a bar-room debate with a buddy about the likely number of yellow cards we thought would be issued by FIFA referees in the forthcoming Football World Cup tournament.

Four years before, 193 yellow cards had been flashed at the 1990 World Cup.

I bet high, he bet low, at £10 per card on either side of the previous 193 yellow cards.

In the end, there were 235 yellow cards issued by World Cup referees, meaning that my buddy owed me £420. When the cheque arrived by post to my workplace, I telephoned to thank him for paying.

'It was good of you to remember that bet, Chopper,' I said. Had he not paid I would have put it down to pub-chat and forgotten about it.

'Honour amongst thieves, old boy, honour amongst thieves,' he replied. We laughed heartily.

By the end of 1994, more than three years into my City career, stock markets were growing strongly, such that the Dow Jones Industrial Index had more than doubled from its low point of the 1987 Crash.

I had taken SNC's annual Irish revenues from £45,000 to £1.5 million—a thirty-fold increase—but was taking a daily pill for Irritable Bowel Syndrome and would soon face a surgeon's knife to repair a hiatus hernia—caused by my stomach bulging into my oesophagus as I crouched behind my workstation like a pilot in a Spitfire fighter aircraft.

'How are you, Chris?' said Michael Marks, SNC's Chairman, on my post-op return to work in late January 1995. I had fixed the surgery for early December, so I could recover over Christmas and return to work in the New Year. But the repair required stitches to tighten the base of my gullet, which caused reflux every time I ate solids.

For the first time since my crash more than six years before, I was back on a liquid diet with the consequent impact on my weight.

'You need a holiday in the sun,' he said – not what I had been expecting after a two-month absence.

Soon, I flew off to Barbados, where US television news reported that the Dow Jones Index had broken through 4000. Before the year-end, it crossed 5000, another 25% increase.

Global markets were hot, and the Thundering Herd, a name Merrill Lynch Inc. derived from its bull logo and its huge team of private client stockbrokers, was on the charge.

In the US, Merrill had brought *Wall Street to Main Street*, and planned to do the same in Europe. In July 1995, Merrill acquired SNC for $840m, and in one swoop became the biggest share trading business in Europe.

If the size of a City firm can be measured by its trading floor, SNC's dealing room was the size of a football pitch and the second-floor share trading floor of Merrill Lynch's new London headquarters would later be the size of two pitches.

I was delighted to be part of one of the biggest global investment banks, whose long-term commitment to staff was reflected in its Wall Street nickname, Mother Merrill. It was a term of affection championed by Dan Tully, Merrill's Chairman and CEO, a renowned dual-nationality Irish-American business leader under whose guidance Merrill's share price tripled between 1992 and 1997.

The first three Merrill executives I met on the old SNC trading floor were of Irish extract.

'Kenney, I know a few of your namesakes in Dublin,' I said to Jerry Kenney, a Merrill executive who had managed the SNC acquisition.

'Sheridan, that's another good Leinster name,' I said to Ed

Sheridan, Head of Global Sales.

'McCann, from outside Belfast,' said Bob McCann before I could venture a guess at his Ulster ancestry.

He would later add Irish citizenship to his US birthright, and six years after would be a contender to lead Merrill Inc., when he sought to follow in the footsteps of Dan Tully and another from the Irish diaspora, Donald Regan, whom as US Treasury Secretary in Ronald Reagan's White House was a leading advocate of Reaganomics.

'Chris, can you pop into my office?' said Brad, my new Head of Sales at Merrill.

'Yes, shortly Brad, if that's okay? I'm busy with client business right now.'

It was not long before the phone rang again, and I was ordered into his office. Brad was a classic American executive: tall, fit and tanned, with as one colleague observed, 'a full head of his own hair'; necessary prerequisites for success in a 'bulge-bracket' financial firm.

'What is it?' I said, hoping to end the chat quickly and get back to business.

'Sit down,' he said. 'I have some good news for you. I'm told that you are Paul Roy's protégé and we want to reward your talent appropriately. We would like to offer you some Merrill stock, as a sign of our faith in your future at the firm.'

'How much do I have to put in?' I asked, presuming some sort of part-payment.

'Nothing,' said Brad with a giggle, 'we're going to give you shares by way of a Golden Hello.'

'Very good!' I replied.

Brad then exaggeratedly scrolled down the lines on a page in front of him, looking for my name on a list. In doing so, he dropped his head and reading spectacles close to the page, so I found myself focusing on his thick, brown mane. He was in his fifties, but without one grey hair. A wig? I wondered.

A toupée?

By the time he looked up from the page, I was struggling to restrain a giggle. The *little devil* from my cerebral contusion was laughing out loud, and when Brad looked up, I found it almost impossible to keep a straight face.

Don't be an idiot! I chastened the laughing boy inside and moved to stand by the door of his small office as Brad prepared to reveal the figure.

'$75,000 of free Merrill Lynch shares,' he said. 'What do you think of that?'

I could not open my mouth for fear of the little devil escaping, so I mumbled, 'Okay, fine,' and quickly left the room, before bursting into laughter on the other side of the door.

'Chris, could you come to my office—now,' said Brad, one day later, and I rushed to do so.

'What is it?' I said, with my best poker face.

This time he sat back in his chair and gave me a stern, schoolmaster's look.

'I want to talk with you about your response to yesterday's offer.'

'Okay,' I said, clamping my emotions.

'I've discussed it with the guys in New York and we've decided to increase the offer to $150,000. You're a valuable member of the team, and we don't want anyone *turning your head*,' he continued, a comment that suggested that I might consider leaving the firm.

'I'm really pleased,' I said, unblinking. 'You can rely on me. I won't be going anywhere.'

'That's good,' said Brad with a smile.

Be bullish was a strapline on Merrill adverts, and I was.

I had moved from being a star striker of a top football league club, to be a star striker at the best club in the world.

Word in our dealing room was that brokers like me were

earning $1m at our New York office, and I saw no reason why I could not do that.

By then, the late summer of 1995, the hosepipe ban affecting many parts of the UK ensured 'firm' ground conditions at most UK racecourses, providing a wonderful opportunity for me. Hard ground conditions and a thoroughbred's brittle legs meant that race field sizes were small. The formula was simple: bet on the short-priced favourites in races with a few runners. I racked up a series of twelve consecutive wins. But this winning run was enough to result in me being banned by William Hill bookmakers.

Hello, my account number is 90489L4,' I said to the telephonist on the betting line. 'I'll have £2000 win on the favourite…' I began, before being interrupted.

'I'm sorry sir, but I cannot take your bet. Please wait while I talk with a manager.'

'Hello, Mr. McGale,' said the second voice, 'we have decided to close your account.'

'Why?' I said, bemused.

'Because your account is *uneconomic*,' he continued.

'Can you do that?' I followed, hoping that I might appeal.

'Yes, we can. Enjoy the rest of your day.'

Soon afterwards, I gave a nickname to my super-fast, cash-purchased, £20,000 BMW 318is turbo: William.

Just as many City colleagues would slip off to a golf course in sleek cars on weekend mornings, my Saturdays began like any other day, analysing and interpreting data before forming firm conclusions.

My working Saturday began at 7am with the Sky and then Channel 4 racing programmes, when I would already be armed with the home-delivered *Racing Post* newspaper and a weekly edition of *Timeform*—a horseracing bible for serious punters.

On one such Saturday morning, February 18, 1995, I took

a train to Windsor for the races, having collected a female companion at Paddington station. Niamh and I had worked at UIB in Dublin and got together after I sought her phone number from her best friend's future husband, another City guy.

Arriving early at Windsor Racecourse, we walked along the beautiful Thames-side figure-of-eight track, talking about happy days in Dublin, and went our separate ways at Paddington.

In Dublin, Niamh had known me in a dealing room environment, exhibiting a serious demeanour as I ground my way through research reports and bought and sold shares for our pension fund clients. But while she had no concept of my gambling life, the form-studying and risk-taking aspects of that were familiar factors for us both.

One week later, as I basked in the Bajan sun far from the colts and fillies of UK racetracks, Niamh was the only thing on my mind.

Later that year, she joined me for a weekend at Dublin's Shelbourne Hotel, where the Saturday morning analysis continued. I selected four horses running at various English racetracks that day and placed my bets via the hotel-room telephone.

Then, while Niamh met friends, I proceeded to a Ladbroke's shop to watch my charges run. I had laid £1000 on the outcome; four £200 trebles, and a £200 accumulator. When the last of the four horses had won, a branch teller calculated electronically my precise winnings: £35,000.

I was, in the words of an Omagh elder whom I advised on horseracing opportunities, winning and losing more every week than the price of a small house in Omagh.

It was now twenty years since I first wanted to be Barney Curley, and I was at the peak of my gambling powers, when I was offered a place at an exclusive poker game played weekly at the Hilton Hotel, Watford. There was a whisper that I had taken a seat once occupied by a well-known footballer who had gone into rehab for problems with booze and gambling, but everyone kept *schtum*.

Around the table were smart players. Two were odds-setters for a major spread betting firm, two had for years travelled from Brighton for the game, two were brothers, and of those six, two went on to play live on TV at the World Series of Poker (WSOP) competition.

We played from 7pm to midnight and each player had to bring a minimum of £5,000 in cash, but most of the seven brought along more, so that there was at least £50,000 cash in the room.

The cash was converted into plastic chips, the most valuable of which, for £1000, was known as a jib. In addition, more chips were issued on guarantees secured from winning players, such that the total amount won and lost on a night could be £100,000.

After three teetotal nights I had accumulated winnings of twelve jibs: £12,000.

It had been a long day at the office, and I ordered a double G&T on arrival at the hotel, as well as another to take with me to the locked meeting room where the game would take place. Two double gin and tonics ran the risk of dulling my senses when I needed to be razor sharp.

'I'll raise you five jibs,' I recounted the words of one of the betting oddsmakers.

It was after 1am and I was sitting on the living room floor of my Hammersmith flat with another large G&T in my hand, searching to no avail for a late-night television programme.

'They were bloody expensive G&Ts,' my inner self said sternly to the image reflected from the TV screen, as I read the news script from Teletext to clear my head.

'Jesus Christ!' I shot back, 'it could have been a lot worse, and two G&Ts didn't make any difference.'

'Are you sure about that?' intoned my alter ego.

With one hour left in the game I had been losing £39,000. I had been struggling all night and took too many risks. I called the £5000 raise in a £20,000 pot and lost. When the chips were counted, I had reduced my losses to £30,000.

I had lost my £5000 cash and owed another £25,000 to winning players.

'Look, you have lost £18,000 overall, not the end of the world,' said a voice of reason.

The pressure was easing; it was time for bed. My daily minicab driver would arrive in a few hours to drive me to The City.

Winning or losing £5,000 on a horse race didn't cause me too much concern, and finding the right race, and the right horse, was always foremost in my mind. But that was different to chucking £39,000 onto a poker table nearly twenty hours after getting up for work the morning before.

It was time to retire, to bed, and from poker.

I had played at the *big table* and never played another game in my life. I had nothing to prove. Poker was just a distraction to my ambition to earn one-million-dollars a year at Merrill.

I first met Dan Tully a few months later, in September 1995. I had flown in from a day trip to Dublin and was among the last to arrive at the Merrill Lynch & Co. Inc. and Smith New Court Plc. merger party.

'Wow, that's amazing,' I said to my Merrill research-colleague as we arrived from the stairwell onto the fourth-floor gallery of the Royal Albert Hall. We were looking down at a sea of more than 5000 red seats in the empty auditorium below.

Ahead I could see the crowds of colleagues attending our

corporate marriage celebration, preceded by the huge frames of two Merrill executives flanked, like steppingstones, by our leaders, Michael Marks, and Paul Roy.

'Dan Tully and Dave Komansky,' I said to my colleague as we made our way past a string quartet towards the human twin towers.

'Hi pal, welcome to Merrill,' said Dan, handing my colleague a Perspex tombstone depicting our mutual symbols, the Merrill bull and the SNC lion, before ushering him on towards Dave. His was one of several hundred hands Dan and Dave had shaken that day.

'Dan, this is Chris McGale,' said Paul.

'Ah, Chris, I have heard a lot about you, and look forward to working with you in Ireland.'

Dan leaned down towards me as he talked and held the handshake as I searched for the right words. The rush there had left me unprepared.

'Thanks Dan, a colleague says it will be *McGale and Lynch* in Ireland,' I said finally, an attempt at humour that fell flat with a man who had already spent forty years at *Merrill Lynch*.

'Okay, pal, we'll talk later.' I too was gifted the tombstone and ushered towards Dave.

But I need not have worried about fluffing my lines with the maestro, and our Irish business boomed as my clients embraced our expanded offer.

Merrill ownership brought with it fantastic franchises in global markets and investment banking, and our UK institutional equities business soon topped the key sectors in the annual Extel survey of City firms.

We were officially the number one UK firm in equities sales, research, sales trading, and trading. In poker terms, we had a full house.

The Dow Jones Index had crossed 4400, having risen 10%

since my Bajan holiday six months before, and would rise nearly 40% that year.

I was happily under the wing of Mother Merrill and would soon earn $300,000. And I didn't need the distraction of poker; a better distraction had emerged in the months since my Caribbean holiday. I was in love.

Niamh and me, Ascot Racecourse, 1996

CHAPTER TWENTY

Lion King

I had wooed Niamh after our day at Windsor races and we had been together for months when in February 1996 we flew to Thailand on holiday. After changing planes in Bangkok, we arrived in Koh Samui before breakfast, eighteen hours after we had set off from London.

On the hotel minibus we met other couples, some of whom Niamh would meet by the sea later that morning and afternoon. After breakfast, I went to bed and slept right through until the following morning, twenty hours later.

After our first day on the beach we watched the *Lion King* movie in our room. I had heard about the Disney animated musical hit that I understood to be a kids' movie.

It was with great embarrassment that we watched the cartoon characters and I struggled to hold back tears in front of my new-found love.

My luck had finally turned for the better.

'I'll lay Frank Bruno at 5/1 for one hundred pounds!' I declared shortly afterwards, happy to risk a few grand to a group of market maker buddies. Bruno had been the WBC champion for eighteen months and was set to put his title on the line against Mike Tyson who had been released from jail a year earlier after serving nearly half of a six-year rape sentence. Tyson had stopped Bruno in Round Five of another World Title clash seven years before.

'You're a fucking, bullshit, wanker,' exclaimed a trader with whom I had not intended to engage.

His ravenous anger raised the same venom in me, in a way that I had not experienced in years.

'For you Steve, the bet is 10/1 for one-thousand-pounds – all or nothing,' I replied with all the calm I could muster. There was silence all around. Would he take the bet? Would he step forward and punch me? And then he skulked back to his workstation, muttering further insults to ripples of muffled laughter around the dealing room.

'You'll like this book, *Angela's Ashes*,' said an Irish American colleague twelve months later.

'What's it about?'

'An impoverished Irish family in New York and Limerick.'

'Sounds like fun!'

'Really, read it. It's one of the best books I have ever read.'

'I rarely read books, but I'm going to Stamford next week, so I'll read it on the plane.'

It was early 1997, and I had read little of Frank McCourt's autobiography by the time I landed at LaGuardia Airport, New York, on my way to a management conference at Merrill's huge complex at Stamford, Connecticut.

Having flown business class from London, I was alone in the back of an air-conditioned limo, reading the story of the terrible afflictions suffered by the McCourt children.

Then it happened, and I put the book face down on the seat beside me. The death of seven-week-old Margaret hit me like a hammer.

Tony Blair's landslide UK Election victory of May 1997 also hit me like a hammer; it proved to be a very costly spread bet.

Five years before, on the morning of the 1992 Election, I

had bet on a Conservative Party victory at winning odds of 7/1 and bought 'futures' on a positive post-election outcome for the FTSE. My win, reported in a newspaper column under the heading *Major Coup*, after the new Prime Minister John Major, netted me £5000.

Despite New Labour's mounting popularity, I had started shorting the size of the likely Blair majority not long after Niamh and I returned from Easter in Barbados where we had seen Luciano Pavarotti perform live at the open-air amphitheatre in the grounds of Holder's Plantation House.

I was sure the youthful, forty-three-year-old Tony Blair would defeat John Major, but felt that there would be no Labour landslide. The landslide forecast by pollsters turned into a tsunami.

Labour's deficit versus the Tories in 1992 was 70 seats, and I bet that Labour would not have a lead over the Tories of more than 150, a huge 220-seat turnaround, and more than a third of all the 650 parliamentary seats.

But as I watched Labour Party celebrations at London's Festival Hall in the early hours of May 2, 1997, my worst fears were realised.

The final Labour lead over the Tories would be declared later that day at 253. At £500 per seat, the 103-seat difference between the 150 seats that I bet low on, and the outcome, cost me £51,500.

My loss had increased on an almost daily basis over a six-week period, throughout the 1997 Election campaign.

I could have stopped the widening chasm at any time by closing the bet. But to do that would have meant crystallising the loss, which I was reluctant to do. So, against my better judgement, I stayed with it until the last vote was counted.

It was a long, expensive, 'pain trade'.

When it was all over, I raised a late-night glass to Tony Blair as he celebrated to the strains of D-Ream's *Things Can Only Get Better*, and would soon be on my way to the office for another day in The City. I was glad that the loss was contained at around £50,000, as I had made an offer of £565,000 on an Edwardian house in Chiswick, West London.

In Wall Street terms, that was nearly one million dollars. But my biggest trade had yet to come.

'That's a fantastic trade, Chris,' said Michael Marks on a now-rare excursion to the trading floor.

'One billion dollars,' I said, 'and a million in fees.' I had made a spectacularly good start to 1998.

'Merrill's biggest ever European *transition trade*,' said Michael, confirming what I knew.

The trade resulted from the acquisition of one asset manager by another, and the resulting consolidation of the two share portfolios.

'Yes, 250 shareholdings sold, consolidated into less than 100 new stocks, to mirror the buyer's portfolio,' I replied.

'Shall I arrange a tombstone to mark the deal?' said Michael.

'Let me ask the client first,' I said, guessing that they would prefer the blockbuster trade to remain anonymous.

Ten years after my accident, for the second time, there was to be no tombstone for me.

Life was good. I had the billion-dollar trade, a million-dollar fee, the million-dollar house, and would soon have the million-dollar wife.

It is every man's dream to fly to a Caribbean island on a supersonic jet with a beautiful girl. Fun to set off on Concorde for Barbados at 10am and arrive at 8am the same day.

Wonderful to quaff champagne and drink fine wines on board.

Delightful to sip more champagne in a chauffeur-driven limo and glide past the coconut trees and corn fields en route to Barbados' exclusive Sandy Lane Hotel.

Heavenly to stand at the altar, best man alongside, and feel the soft sea air from the steel blue waters of the Caribbean

Sea blow through the open windows.

A dream to wait in the quiet, save for a flautist's soft air, until the sparkling girl in the Versace dress arrived on her father's arm.

It was a dream I had never dreamed; I was living it.

Niamh and I were married in Barbados at the Church of St Francis of Assisi on Thursday, April 23, 1998, surrounded by family and friends from Omagh, Wexford and Dublin. My wife's brother, a priest, performed the ceremony with the permission of the Bishop of Bridgetown.

Everyone stayed at sea-front hotels along a stretch of Barbados coast known as St James'. To avoid the morning heat, the wedding was scheduled for 3pm, and after the service we returned to the Sandy Lane for champagne and canapés on the roof terrace.

The wedding party then went to the wonderful Cliff Restaurant, where the setting really lives up to its name. I was on first-name terms with the owner and was usually allocated the prime seafront dinner table; except when Puff Daddy's reservation shifted us to a table beside him.

Hotel Bel-Air, Beverley Hills, Los Angeles, was the next stop for Niamh and me—a delightful place associated with The Oscars ceremony.

The concierge arranged a dinner table at Spago's Restaurant on Sunset Boulevard, where we dined alongside screen legend Tony Curtis and his tall, blonde, wife-to-be Jill Vandenberg. Curtis received a standing ovation on arrival.

We visited the Gucci store on Rodeo Drive that was once owned by an Irish company I invested in, Power Corporation. We would soon make our way to San Francisco, as we were now in the third week of a month-long honeymoon, and then planned to visit Las Vegas.

Awake at dawn one morning, I went outside the Bel-Air complex for a walk as the sun rose on Stone Canyon

Road and met mostly Hispanic manual workers manicuring already pristine lawns and hedgerows. I wondered how many generations of change would pass before these workers would leave behind their life of toil.

I was listening on audiotape to Jung Chang's *Wild Swans: Three Daughters of China*—a story about the struggle of three generations of women in twentieth-century China. It was apposite. There would be no more manual labour, no more struggles, and no more strife. I had left it all behind, I had escaped.

I was a member of Crockfords Club, the exclusive London casino, as SNC had been its City advisor, but had little interest in blackjack, and never played roulette or slot machines. On my walk I decided that we would not be going to Vegas and knew that my wife would be happy with that.

I was also a member at Ascot, where we looked forward to attending the week-long Royal Ascot racing festival in a month's time. A few days later Niamh and I were at Newbury Racecourse having flown to London via San Francisco.

We joined partners in Merlyn Racing, the Merrill Lynch racing syndicate, to celebrate our nuptials and watch what transpired to be our slow racehorse Guildhall.

Paul Roy, now riding high at Merrill Lynch, had become a reluctant member of the Merlyn syndicate, paying the joining fee, after an entreaty by the top revenue generator in his team, me. 'Suzanne, please come in here,' he said to his PA via an intercom. 'Give this guy a cheque for £10,000 and get him out of here!'

Dashing Dollar, our first horse, was a nervous beast by the time he arrived from Ireland. After a few bad races we sent him to convalesce at our trainer's parents' West Country farm where he was at home in a field with ducks and geese. It was an inauspicious start for the syndicate, and one partner succinctly renamed our charge Crashing Dollar.

But we remained an enthusiastic group of owners, often

making our way to the Lambourn training complex to watch Guildhall at early morning Saturday gallops.

At Newbury, our horse's handlers were keen to keep onside the group of City high rollers and sought to impress after Guildhall was beaten twenty-five lengths when finishing last of seven runners in the second race.

He had previously finished third of four runners on our wedding day more than three weeks before.

'My girlfriend is best friends with a girl at Henry Cecil's yard,' said our horse's groom.

'Really?' I said, my antenna spiking.

'She says that Bold Fact will win the 3.45 race at Newmarket.'

'Perfect,' I said. 'He's a good horse Bold Fact, would you like a glass of champagne?'

Tipping a horse that was well fancied in the morning press from a leading trainer was not what I would call a tip. But it did remind me not to forget to bet on him.

'Royal Anthem,' he continued. 'You should back him too, a three-year-old newcomer running in the last race here today.'

My day had started well when I put £1000 on Frankie Dettori's mount in the first race at odds of 6/1. A star jockey like Dettori riding for a local trainer at Newbury was the clue, and the horse ran out an easy winner.

'How are you getting on?' I said to a random punter in the champagne bar two hours later.

'Not great,' said the grey-suited stranger, 'but I've got a tip for later!'

'It's just as well that you reminded me,' I said. 'I have a tip running in a few minutes. In fact, I have two, one running later at Newmarket, and Cecil's three-year-old in the last race here. Royal Anthem,' I said, 'will soon be off to Royal Ascot and so will I.'

I deposited a haul of bubbly with my syndicate partners and hurried to an on-track betting shop to check the odds.

'Put £20 on Bold Fact for me,' said a friend as I left, which I did at the on-course betting shop at odds of 3/1.

'I'll have £3,000 win on Bold Fact at 3/1 in the 3.45 at Newmarket,' I said to Martin Densham, my personal bookie, who was at the top end of a long row of 'open-outcry' oddsmakers. 'And a £500 treble on Bold Fact at 3/1, plus starting prices on Royal Anthem in the 4.35 here, and Churlish Charm in the 4.45 at Newmarket,' I continued.

'Sorry Chris, Bold Fact is now 11/4,' said Martin, after checking the odds via his mobile phone.

'Okay, no worries, make that a four-grand win, and a £600 treble.'

I liked to bet in what I called 'round numbers,' wholes and halves, not quarters and eighths, and so the bets became £4000 and £600 rather than £3000 and £500.

The decision to add another grand on Bold Fact added two-grand to my winnings, but to bet £600 rather than £500 on the treble proved to be worth more than £10,000, when one hour later Churlish Charm crossed the line to win the last race at Newmarket.

We cheered the winner on a television monitor in the now-deserted Newbury Racecourse grandstand, having done the same outside 10 minutes earlier, when Royal Anthem won the last race at Newbury by an easy 3-lengths. Both were priced at the generous odds of 9/2.

The £600 treble was worth £68,000, versus £57,000 for a £500 bet, and I was already winning £26,000. As well as Dettori's winner in the first race, I had bet another £2000 on Royal Anthem at 9/2. My total win was £94,000.

But in the final push for the finish line, Churlish Charm had cut across the runner up, a manoeuvre for which his jockey later received a 2-day ban for 'careless riding.'

When the Stewards Enquiry was announced into the jockey's riding, I knew that disqualification would cost me

£68,000.

'I see you had a good result,' said Martin Densham, whose father Pat had named the Sunderland's bookie business after the aeroplane he had flown in, as a rear-gunner in World War II.

'Yes, but there's an objection against the winner at Newmarket.'

'I'm on the M4 on my way home,' he said, 'and I haven't seen the race. But I'll give you an even ten-grand on the other horse in the inquiry.'

'Okay, I'll have £10,000 on the second horse to win the objection,' I said instantly.

'It's a hedge,' I explained to a Merlyn Racing partner while we waited on the judges. 'I've put ten-grand on the second horse to maximise my downside. I'll win £36,000, if the objection goes against me, or £84,000 if my horse keeps the race.'

Soon, I lost the fastest ten grand I had ever lost on a horserace, in return for my biggest ever win on a day. It was a perfect way to end the third week of our month-long honeymoon.

Having lost fifty-grand going short on Labour in the general election twelve months before, I didn't hesitate to go short again after reading in a morning newspaper about the number of red cards forecast in the 1998 football World Cup.

I had made £420 being long yellow cards four years before and had read over Saturday breakfast about FIFA's desire for referees to become much stricter on dangerous tackles.

The number of teams competing had increased from 24 to 32, and the number of matches to be played rose from 52 to 64, so the number of Red Cards would logically rise. With tighter rules on dangerous tackles, and far more teams and matches, spread betters anticipated a surge in red cards.

Surely not three and a half times the fifteen red cards that were issued in the tournament four years before? I mused, and went short £500 per card, at 51 cards.

There were no red cards in the opening games and the odds tumbled into the low teens, where I continued to short with different spread betting bookies, at £500 per card on a further eight occasions, until the bet had increased to £4500 per card, with a card average of 27.5.

By the halfway stage, twelve red cards had been issued in the thirty-two matches that had already been played, with another thirty-two matches still to play. Oddsmakers were now expecting the final 'make up' to be 24 cards, that would mean a win of nearly £16,000 for me, but with four games being played every day, the pressure was unrelenting.

My body convulsed and a wreath of shingles wrapped around my midriff when the referee issued a straight red card to Scotland's Craig Burley. It was around 9pm and I was alone in my living room watching a game of football I cared little about, except for the financial liability it represented.

The red card was the third of the day, as two Cameroonian players had been sent off in an earlier match I had watched with faux indifference at my workplace. That meant the red card total was now 15 after 36 matches, the same number that had been issued in the entire 52-match tournament four years before.

Red card issuance was accelerating, and the ratio of red cards to games that day was three-in-four. Had it continued at that rate, with 28 matches still to play, the count would have reached 36, and resulted in a loss for me of more than £38,000.

But like the Blair landslide, when I didn't cut the hopeless trade, I decided to 'take the pain.'

Fortunately, the card count slowed to one-in-four matches and by the tournament end, 22 red cards had been issued, resulting in a win of nearly £25,000.

There was no celebration on my part, just disappointment that Marcel Desailly got sent off in the Final, costing me £4,500, and relief that another *pain trade* was over.

Gambling had destroyed any love I had for sport.

'Chris, do you think you should stop gambling?' said my new wife a short time later.

'Nah, I have won £100,000 in recent weeks, why would I stop?'

'The pressure of that, and work, will kill you, and it's a huge distraction from your City job.'

I agreed with that as I had never been busier at work.

'Would you try Gamblers Anonymous?

'You're joking, aren't you?'

'No, I'm deadly serious.'

I knew she was right, I needed to stop gambling.

There were many days when I would go to the pub after work and then stop off in a betting shop and bet on horseraces in five grand clips. All my hard-wrought discipline had gone.

The Gamblers Anonymous meeting started badly. I was reminded of an Al-Anon meeting I attended as a teenager, when Paul first went into Alcohol Rehab nearly twenty years before.

That was his problem, not mine, and I never attended another meeting.

'Why did you come here today?' said Jack, the white-haired elder statesman of the group of males I had joined.

'I need to stop gambling.'

'Is gambling causing you difficulties, distress?'

'Yes and no. I've been gambling all my life and I'm good at it, but I'm busy with work, and it's a huge distraction.'

'So, you've been losing recently?' said Jack.

'No, that's not the case,' I replied holding back the details as I had by now realised that no one in this group was in my league. No one except Jack that was, and he was keen to get more out of me.

'So why did you come here?'

'I've explained that,' I replied tartly.

'Did you come here because your wife, or family, asked you to?'

'Yes and no,' I said again, putting up a defensive wall.

'Do you think you need help?'

'Yes, to stop.'

'But you say that you're a winning gambler, why do you want to stop?'

'I don't always win, and the sums involved have become ridiculous.'

'I think you're in denial,' he said.

'I don't think I would be sitting here if that were true,' I shot back.

'If you think you're going to win next time, you will never stop,' he countered.

Jack was right. I did believe I would win next time, and never returned to Gamblers Anonymous.

I was now running the 7am morning meeting at Merrill, from the middle of our huge trading floor when several hundred broker, trading, and research colleagues listened via desk-mounted squawk boxes.

We were at the centre of the universe, trading after the close of Asian markets, and before the opening bell on Wall Street.

It was 1998, nearly 10 years after my car crash, and eighteen since I walked into Omagh Tech pleading to go back to school.

I had it all. I had married the girl of my dreams. The Dow Jones Index had crossed 9,000, having more than doubled since Merrill acquired SNC three and a half years before. Our stock price and my salary had also doubled.

It would not be long before I would earn $1m for my year's work at Merrill.

CHAPTER TWENTY-ONE

The Omagh Bomb

'Can you drive a car, son?' said a police officer to my tall fifteen-year-old nephew Stephen.

'No, unfortunately not,' he replied, knowing that he could not help ferry injured bomb victims to the nearby Tyrone County Hospital.

It was Saturday, August 15, 1998, and I had returned home from lunch by the Thames with Niamh and my sister Briegie, when television news bulletins reported that a huge car bomb had exploded in Omagh. The scene was described as a warzone, with reports of many deaths and hundreds of casualties. The blast, the reports said, was likely to be the work of the Real IRA—a Republican splinter group.

Stephen, the youngest son of my eldest sister Marie, and his elder sister Bronagh, my goddaughter, had been among the hundreds of people evacuated from the upper part of Omagh town centre following a telephone bomb warning, which had provided incorrect details of where the bomb had been placed.

They and Ciara, Noelle's, nineteen-year-old eldest child, were among several hundred people to be unintentionally moved towards the bomb by the police, who had cordoned off the High-Street area around the Court House at the top of the town following misleading directions telephoned to the Samaritans and Ulster Television. The bomb they said was in a car parked in Main Street; no such street existed in Omagh.

Men, women, and children who had come to town to buy uniforms for the new school year, continued with their shopping day, as bomb scares were not unusual in Northern Ireland at that time. Many went to Kells clothes shop—a popular retailer of back-to-school wear, outside of which was parked a stolen Vauxhall Cavalier laden with a 500-pound bomb.

The victims were packed around that and other cars waiting expectantly for the security alert to be lifted when the fertiliser-bomb was detonated, at 3.10pm.

Ciara and her friends were on the footpath just a few doors from Kells and felt the full force of the blast. She was thrown up into the air and had a piece of glass lodged above her right eye. Shortly afterwards, one of her girlfriends telephoned Noelle to say that she was okay, but hysterical. Noelle had been distressed at home waiting for Ciara to return her call.

The thunderous noise of the blast and the plume of smoke that engulfed the town could be heard and seen ten miles away. The principal fixed-line telephone cabinet that stood on Market Street was destroyed by the bomb and soon the volume of calls being made would overwhelm the mobile telephone system. That meant that no calls could be made or received, greatly adding to the distress of the huge numbers of people seeking to contact loved ones.

Noelle found the girls at the rear of the buildings were the bomb had been detonated. They had made there way there via an entryway and had been very lucky. At the front of those buildings, Market Street was a scene of carnage.

Thirty-one people died. Three generations of women from one family were killed: a 65-year-old grandmother, her 30-year-old daughter, her 18-month-old granddaughter, and unborn twin granddaughters. The final death toll read: fourteen women, six men, five girls, four boys and unborn twins.

For Noelle, it was the beginning of a long day as an operative at the sterilizing unit at the Tyrone County Hospital. For eighteen of the next twenty-four hours, she worked in what medical staff described as battlefield conditions. One hundred and thirteen people were detained in Omagh and province-wide hospitals overnight and over three hundred were injured.

Two days later, I travelled to Dublin for investor meetings with an executive of the weapons manufacturer, Marconi Plc. When our day of meetings with investment institution was over, I hired a car and drove to Omagh. Like everyone, I was angry and wanted to go there to see it for myself.

But I had learned a long time ago not to cry at someone else's funeral, and after attending just one wake the following day I cut short a planned three-day visit and returned to London.

That night I penned a letter entitled *The Last Atrocity*, which I sent by email to the editors of various UK and Irish newspapers. It was published as the lead letter in the Irish Independent newspaper under the heading: 'Omagh was a good town to grow up in.'

That was part of a quote from the Omagh-born writer Benedict Kiely from a newspaper article I read that day. My letter ended with a quote from another local man with whom I spoke that day: 'That will be the last bomb in Ireland,' he said. It was just four months after the Belfast Agreement had been signed by the warring factions on Good Friday, April 10, 1998.

A few months later, before Christmas, a friend posted to me a video recording of *The Late Late Show*, an Irish television chat show hosted by Gay Byrne. It was dedicated that week to the victims of the Omagh Bomb.

There, on live television, were among the most severely

injured victims of the bomb. One girl was blinded, another wore a plastic mask to cover burns to her face and scalp.

I had more than a little understanding of what they were going through and felt a surge of guilt. What had I done for them? What could I do for them?

I recalled words from an *Ulster Herald* newspaper diary written by my good friend Stephen McKenna on August 20, 1998, five days after the atrocity: *Three funerals virtually overlap in Church Street, Omagh, with a fourth at Drumragh. The fine weather has receded and in the ceaseless rain all nature seems to be in mourning...*

On Saturday, January 9, 1999, Niamh and I flew home to meet with the Head of the Omagh Fund, John McKinney, who was also Omagh District Council's Chief Executive Officer, (CEO).

My proposal was that the corporate sector in which I worked could be further targeted by the Fund and that, as an Omagh native, I had both the capacity and desire to spearhead a fundraising effort.

I offered to take a 12-month sabbatical from Merrill and work unpaid for the Fund.

John explained that there were already council staff working on major fundraising events and had already arranged fundraising football matches between Omagh Town FC, Chelsea, Liverpool, and Man Utd, as well as a 3000-person free concert featuring The Corrs.

He judged correctly that I would be more effective helping the Fund while continuing in my City role. And so, I became the Fund's de facto chief corporate fundraiser, I had no official title, business card or plan, just a desire to get on.

My first task was to accompany John to a London meeting with an executive of Carlton Television Plc., who had made what was widely regarded as a distasteful chat show programme about the bomb; something they later acknowledged.

John outlined the distress the programme had caused to the people of Omagh and I suggested that Carlton should make a public show of contrition that could be satisfied by a donation of £100,000.

We came away with a commitment that the issue would be discussed at Carlton Board level and the Omagh Fund later received a cheque for £30,000.

Flushed with that success, I was soon to take my desire to promote the Fund beyond the realms of professional reason.

It was the spring of 1999, and I was invited by Dan Tully, now Merrill's Chairman Emeritus, who retained a role in Dublin as a Board Member of Merrill Lynch Capital Markets Bank, to join a dinner in Dublin with Tony O'Reilly, the media baron and billionaire entrepreneur who controlled Independent News & Media Plc. (INM).

We dined at O'Reilly's palatial townhouse, joined by his son Gavin, and Brendan Hopkins, who ran the O'Reilly Group's UK media interests. One year before O'Reilly had stepped down from HJ Heinz Inc. where he was the first non-Heinz family member to hold the post of Chairman.

While in the US, he founded and was Chairman of the Ireland Funds—an umbrella group represented internationally by the American Ireland Fund, The Great Britain Fund for Ireland, and others.

I reasoned that the dinner would provide an excellent opportunity to explore how the Omagh Fund could tap into the Ireland Funds' global reach. I had intended to find a suitable moment to raise the subject of Omagh during the evening, but no opportunity arose.

I had brought with me three envelopes to pass to Tony, Gavin, and Brendan, each containing a photocopy of the letter about my day in Omagh that INM's *Irish Independent* newspaper had published. Had the subject of Omagh been discussed over dinner, the letter would underline my commitment to the Fund.

It was only as Dan and I were saying our last goodbyes in the mirrored hallway of the fine Georgian townhouse in Dublin's Fitzwilliam Square that I proffered the envelopes to our hosts and mentioned my involvement with the Omagh Fund.

Having attended many meetings with Dan in the four years since Merrill acquired SNC, I knew immediately that he was not happy.

A self-made Irish American business icon, who started life in a tenement block in New York, Dan was a prolific giver and organiser on behalf of many charities. He was a Board member of the American Ireland Fund, and in a personal capacity had advised Pope John Paul II at the Vatican.

Dan had been the driving force behind the establishment of our Capital Markets Bank, at Dublin's International Financial Services Centre (IFSC), a business that was then generating annual profits of $100m.

'Take your work seriously but never yourself,' scolded Dan later. He embraced and promoted the ideal of Mother Merrill, where you take care of your fellow employees for the good of all.

I had hijacked a Merrill meeting for my own purpose, no matter what the purpose. A less understanding boss would have fired me on the spot.

My effort, however, was not in vain, as Tony promised to put me in touch with the Ireland Funds' top executives.

The Ireland Funds later helped with the 1999 launch of the Omagh Fund CD in the USA, and Tony O'Reilly received an honorary knighthood in the New Year's Honours list of 2000.

When Dan Tully and I visited him at his magnificent residence, Castlemartin House, Kilcullen, Co. Kildare, in the autumn of 2000 we inspected Claude Monet's 'Le Portail (Soleil)', one of more than thirty that Monet painted of Rouen Cathedral between 1892 and 1893. Tony told us that he had recently paid $24m for the impressionist masterpiece at a Sotheby's New York auction, via a telephone bid, and that he had cycled through the city as a teenager.

In September that year, the Ireland Fund of Great Britain donated to the Omagh Fund the £100,000 proceeds from the London premiere of Ben Elton and Andrew Lloyd Webber's new production *The Beautiful Game*, a musical set in troubled Belfast.

In 2002, the Ireland Funds made its largest ever donation of $500,000 towards the creation of a Community House on the rebuilt bomb site.

John Cleese had famously called Gerry Robinson an 'ignorant upstart caterer' following the latter's 1992 appointment as CEO of Granada Group, the UK media company. Gerry, who hailed from Paddy's beloved Dunfanaghy, had previously led a management buyout of Compass Caterers.

By 1999, Gerry was a FTSE 100 superstar, having led Granada's £3.8bn hostile takeover of Forte Hotels Plc. three years before. Later ennobled to Sir Gerry, he was one of Tony Blair's favourite businessmen and had offered to help the Omagh Fund.

Together we formed the Friends of Omagh, London, a group that consisted of him and me. Our sole objective was to organise a lunch in London to be hosted by Tony Blair. I was also on the Board of the Friends of Omagh, Dublin, a group numbering ten Irish corporate executives.

At the first meeting, Philip Lynch, CEO, IAWS Plc., offered to make available for resale three of the four races that his firm had sponsored at the Curragh Racecourse on the day before the Irish Derby, Saturday June 26th, 1999. At €15,000 each, that generated €45,000.

The racecourse management provided, free-of-charge, the forty-seat Nijinsky Suite for the new race-day sponsors, where one lunch guest promised a substantial contribution to the Fund from the proceeds of the sale of a prized goat.

Our day ended when John McKinney and I joined Philip and two hundred IAWS staff with their partners at a racecourse marquee. They had donated the entire €150,000 proceeds of the IAWS Staff Charity Scheme to the Omagh Fund.

When Gerry Robinson and I met in London to discuss the proposed lunch with Tony Blair, he showed me a long list of potential media and City guests, including Richard Branson and Tony O'Reilly.

We would target them at a cost of £25,000 per seat. Gerry delivered most of the guest list and I wrote the letter to be sent to potential attendees. The last line read: 'Remember, you can make a difference.'

Our target for the final twelve lunch attendees that we hoped would 'make a difference' was £300,000.

The Blair lunch took place at the Grosvenor House Hotel on July 26th, 1999, a few weeks before the first anniversary of the bomb. Although we had targeted twelve attendees, we sent out twenty-five invitations and had an incredible twenty-two positive responses. With £10,000 contributed by two non-attendees, the event raised £560,000 for the Omagh Fund.

Merrill chose to send a senior media investment-banking colleague instead of me, but I was keen to attend. When I broached with Niamh the question of me paying the £25,000 ticket price, her response was to ask why I had got involved in the fundraising exercise in the first place. Was it 'to sit at lunch with Tony Blair?' The lunch went ahead without me.

Seats were also at a premium for lunch with An Taoiseach, Bertie Ahern, which John attended on behalf of the Fund.

'Who's going to get us started?' said Bertie. 'It would be too bad if we couldn't do better than Blair!' One guest pitched onto the table a cheque for €100,000 and others followed until the Taoiseach's assembled guests did 'do better than Blair', raising €800,000.

Three pre-teenage boys from Buncrana, Co. Donegal, died in the Omagh Bomb. Also murdered was a twelve-year-old boy, and a twenty-three-year-old female youth-leader, from Madrid, Spain. They were part of a language exchange programme with Buncrana Primary School and had travelled to Omagh for a shopping day.

Across the Bridge of Hope is the title of the Omagh Fund CD. Its name was taken from a line in *The Bridge*, a poem of peace penned by one of the boys, Seán McLaughlin, and sent to the Irish President, Mary McAleese, shortly before he perished. On the Omagh Fund CD, Liam Neeson reads *The Bridge* beautifully:

The Bridge
Orange and green, it does not matter.
United now, don't shatter our dream.
Scatter the seeds of peace over our land,
So we can travel, hand in hand,
Across the bridge of hope.
Seán McLaughlin (*age 12, summer 1998*)

The CD featured contributions from most of the major Irish artists, including Boyzone, Daniel O'Donnell, Enya, Paul Brady, Sinead O'Connor, Snow Patrol, The Corrs, U2, and Van Morrison.

Despite the quality of the offering, its arrival in the pre-Christmas 1998 market meant global distributors did not pick it up. It flopped, and a large block of unsold CDs remained in a Belfast warehouse.

And so, I set out to raise $50,000 for the CD's launch in the USA. To senior colleagues I offered blocks of 50 CDs at £1,000 and sold individual CDs for £10 in the foyers of Merrill's three main London offices. Everyone from temporary secretaries to porters and managing directors wanted to help and the money was raised with ease.

Seamus Heaney's, The Cure at Troy, was also read on the CD by Liam Neeson, something I had done at the 1998 Merrill Lynch Christmas Party at a Dublin restaurant. I had photocopied a newspaper article on Heaney's verse adaptation of Sophocles' play Philoctetes to read on the flight to Dublin and was blown away by the Nobel Laureate's words; when hope and history rhyme.

It was a year that contained both the Good Friday Agreement and four months later the Omagh Bomb. When a party-making London colleague suggested that all twenty attendees take turns at relating a funny story or something about themselves, I read from the photocopy but not in a party way.

My reading engendered a mixed response; some clearly thought I was mad. The verse talks of *wrongs inflicted and endured, of the longed-for tidal wave of justice, rising up, and of miracles, hope and healing wells, when hope and history rhyme*. For me, it represented the newfound but fragile peace and exhibited the soreness, after the conflict.

The war was over.

My association with the Omagh Fund came to an end at Christmas 2000, when Niamh and I attended an event hosted by the Irish President, Mary McAleese, at Áras an Uachtaráin. The event was arranged by John to thank the emergency services and those who had helped on the day and in the aftermath.

In the more than two years since the atrocity, John had worked tirelessly on behalf of the Fund for the victims and their families, and for Omagh town. On that night, he had every right to feel proud that the Fund had closed with donations received to the value of £6.7 million.

When we arrived at the President's Phoenix Park residence, the Dublin minicab driver, who could not help but hear our conversation, refused to accept any payment for the journey.

The guests covered a wide spectrum from the Omagh area police chief, to firefighters, surgeons, doctors, nurses, and other heroes of the day.

Among the attendees was a local solicitor who was also the Omagh coroner. She related to me the horrific tale of how she had spent several days with the bodies in a makeshift morgue at the town's St. Lucia Barracks.

She had collected ground rents from me on behalf of Omagh's Molly Hughes estate and knew nothing of my involvement with the Fund. Few did, as my fundraising efforts were focused outside Omagh and I never met any of the injured victims.

The Dublin event was symbolic of the wider peace that had taken hold in Northern Ireland following the Good Friday Agreement, after three decades of The Troubles.

In attendance was Detective Chief Inspector James Baxter, whom I had not previously met, but with whom I had a warm exchange. Nine years after my Dundalk court case, I knew that he would not lightly have made the decision to cross the border.

The war was over.

'The old man would like a word,' said Gavin O'Reilly and handed me his cell phone. I had spent the day with Gavin and the management of iTouch, an Independent News & Media subsidiary that offered internet services via mobile phones, which Merrill was helping Tony O'Reilly float in London.

It was the tail-end of the five-year dotcom bubble, March 31, 2000, with investors becoming increasingly sceptical of dotcom Initial Public Offering (IPO) opportunities. iTouch would have £1m in sales in the half year to June 2000, but we managed to float 25% of the company in August at a £200m valuation, half the valuation targeted in March, but enough to allow it to list on the LSE. During the intervening five-month period, British 'dotcom darlings' like *boo.com* and *lastminute.com* had become 'dotcom dogs.'

'Thank you, Chris, Gavin says you have been doing a great job,' said Tony.

'We still have some way to go Tony, but I think we'll get the deal done.'

'Very good,' he said. 'Chryss and I are having a party tomorrow night at Castlemartin. Can you and your wife come over, and stay with us? And it would be great if you could be my guest at the Ireland v Wales match in the afternoon.'

Tony, now Sir Anthony, for his 'long and distinguished service to Northern Ireland,' was at that time negotiating to buy the Belfast Telegraph. Also at the pre-match lunch table under the Lansdowne Road, West Stand, were Lord Laird, founding Chairman of the Ulster-Scots Agency, set up two years before as part of the Good Friday Agreement, and seated next to me Ken Maginnis, Ulster Unionist MP for Fermanagh and South Tyrone, with whom I had a convivial conversation about his playing days at Dungannon Rugby Club.

The tribal conflict meant that rugby and soccer were considered 'foreign games' at my schools, and I had never played nor had seen a live game of rugby, other than internationals at Twickenham and Lansdowne, and the bonhomie ended when I related my earliest memory of The Troubles thirty years before.

I told Ken of civil rights protestors being beaten on John Street Corner by baton-wielding officers of the B-Specials. 'We shall overcome,' they sang, in the streets below us before the mayhem, and then a white-shirted young man with a loudhailer shouted, 'this is a peaceful demonstration, do not retaliate.'

Two of the more seriously injured civilians were dragged into our Kevlin Road hallway, where we children watched from the landing above as our mother tended to their wounds with blood-soaked bar towels, as the pandemonium continued outside.

'That didn't happen,' said Ken, emphatically. It was time to go back to the rugby conversation.

Nine months later at the Omagh Fund event at the President's residence, I made conversation with Highland Radio's Country Music DJ, and community stalwart, Pio McCann, whom I knew from Mum's days at the pub. I asked him if he knew who I was.

'I'm Chris McGale,' I said, after it became clear that he didn't.

'Ah, Chris!' he said, and broke into a volume of praise about the wonderful woman mum was. His face lit up at the memory. It was Kate McGale this, and Kate McGale that.

I had often talked with Niamh about Mum, but that spontaneous outpouring helped her understand the esteem in which she was held, more than any words from me could ever do. And Niamh was now four months pregnant with the next Kate McGale.

President McAleese, whose family was one of 2000 mostly-Catholic families forced out of their Belfast homes with fire and gunfire, at the same time as the B-Specials were battering civil rights protesters in Omagh thirty years before, offered words of support and consolation to the departing guests at the top of the long-stairs exit at Áras an Uachtaráin.

She said to me that Omagh needed an ambassador like John Hume in Derry, for whose SDLP Party, my Queen's University English-Masters-graduate-nephew, Stephen, mentioned earlier on the day of the Omagh Bomb, would later become Communications Officer. But my time helping the Omagh Fund had come to an end, and the challenge of championing the town was a job for elected members and officials, not me.

Copy of signatories to Belfast Agreement, Good Friday, 1998, given to me by Philip Lynch, CEO, IAWS Plc., and Board member, Friends of Omagh, Dublin.

CHAPTER TWENTY-TWO

Tech Crash

My sabbatical offer at the start of 1999 coincided with record stock market levels after four consecutive double-digit annual gains on the Dow Jones Index.

My client revenues were now more than five times what I generated at SNC three and a half years before, rising from $2m to $11m.

Despite my dollar success, I didn't reveal my sabbatical proposal to anyone at Merrill, as my relationship with Brad could now be compared with our slow racehorse, Crashing Dollar.

Russian Flu, a name given to the Russian Debt crisis of 1998, was speculated to have caused an existential scare to Merrill. That led to a collective belt-tightening across the firm and a new regime in London, with Brad cracking the whip as he sought to control self-doers like me.

It would prove to be the beginning of the end of Dan Tully's beloved Mother Merrill, and for me.

To Brad's great frustration I had been untouchable. As a big-hitter, I had, in the first years under Merrill, been left to my own devices, just as I had under SNC's management in the four years before that, when I proudly boasted the firm's biggest monthly expense bill.

As my Irish business grew strongly, I spent my week going back and forth to Dublin with Merrill analysts and UK corporate executives.

That had caused apparent annoyance to at least one colleague, who in the early days before my revenue line spoke for itself, seemed to constantly whinge about my absences. He had a double-barrelled name and was public school educated, whereas I went to Omagh Tech and felt a certain disdain when in his company. One day, I would no doubt be shown to be the freeloading, company-credit-card wielding, Good-time Charlie, that I felt certain he thought I was, whereas my lack of respect for him as a broker allowed me to ignore him at will.

'I want you to be at the front of the queue, so get in front of the clients as much as possible when markets are quiet, and when things get busy again you'll be at the forefront of their thinking,' Paul Roy had said, when licencing me to go and spend the firm's money.

I had indeed been his protégé and in becoming a huge revenue generator, had more than justified his faith in me. He was also one of the 'significant males' that I looked up to in life and it was unfortunate for the whinger when he entered an elevator that was at that moment being randomly shared by only Paul Roy and me.

'This guy wants to know why I spend so much time in Dublin,' I said to the boss and promptly exited the lift. I never did get to hear what was said after I stepped into the foyer, but I never heard the guy whinge to me again at SNC or Merrill.

'I'm the best signing you ever made,' I once said to Paul Roy. On that day we were hammering the phones, desperately trying to 'place' the remaining block of stock SNC had acquired in a second-tier, FTSE 250, company. It was a risky transaction and failure to sell the shares would cause an 'overhang' in an illiquid name and might cost us hundreds of thousands of pounds. Before I announced that I had in fact placed the last block I beckoned our hovering leader towards my desk and despite knowing that the deal was done, said again to my client so that all could hear, 'so you'll take the final quarter-of-a-million shares?' In the buzz of the moment my 'best signing' hubris that followed caused resounding laughter from my boss and broker colleagues.

Five years later, Merrill was bullish for another good year ahead as we pushed towards the new millennium, and had just hired as our Head of Global Internet Research, Henry Blodget, who had achieved fame by predicting a meteoric rise in the share price of Amazon.com

Amazon had been a public company for only a year in late 1998, when Henry predicted it would rise from its $240 share price to $400 within 12 months. Three weeks later, it zipped through $400 on its way to $500, and soon after, Henry signed for Merrill in a deal reportedly worth $12 million per annum.

There was, said the bulls, a new paradigm driving stocks. The brave new world of technology investment that saw a surge in global Telecoms Media & Technology (TMT) shares, otherwise known as the dotcom bubble.

It was all about content and distribution, said the evangelists, with telecom companies providing the pipes to distribute the media content and internet innovation.

Investment managers who did not buy into the mantra got hammered in the performance tables as internet stocks like Amazon, America Online (AOL), Cisco, Intel, Microsoft, Oracle, and Yahoo soared.

Tech stocks literally went crazy as we raced towards the millennium, and the NASDAQ-100 Index of US tech and other growth stocks, gained 85% in 1999, the biggest annual gain of any major US index in history.

By comparison, despite a Y2K push that would see it finish the year at an all-time high, the 'low-Tech' FTSE 100 recorded an annual gain that year of 18%; a record index level that was not exceeded for another fifteen years.

TMT in Europe was dominated by Telecom giants like Vodafone Airtouch (Vodafone), handset manufacturers like Nokia, Media companies like Gerry Robinson's Granada Media, and BSKYB (Sky) who were cornering Premier League matches for their satellite distribution network. But UK Technology stocks like ARM Holdings were small by comparison.

Merrill stock analysts were City superstars as we had built a team of top-rated researchers in most LSE sectors, including Chemicals, Construction, Financials, Healthcare, Media, Oil & Gas, Property, Support Services, Telecoms, Transport and Utilities.

In the football parlance that I liked to use about our work, being in the Merrill team was like playing for UEFA Champions League Winners, Man United.

Despite constant approaches by head-hunters offering big money deals, I played for Merrill Lynch and had no desire to play anywhere else.

We had all the FTSE star players.

Our analysts were the playmakers who, through their research publications and morning meeting insights, gave the ball to super-striker stockbrokers like me, to inspire idea-hungry asset managers in good time for them to place buy or sell orders with our market makers when trading began at 8am.

As most business was conducted in the morning, and as bedside alarms rang at 5.30am, lunchtime was a welcome distraction, and boozy lunches with clients and colleagues were the norm for many City brokers, and for me.

With our star group of leading research analysts Merrill would soon be corporate advisor to nearly one quarter of the constituents of the FTSE 100, as well as many others in the smaller FTSE 250 Index, and most days finished with follow-up presentations of the research discussed at the morning meeting, or an hour-long corporate briefing.

One of our top analysts was Tam MacStair, a fun-loving Englishman who was proud of his Scottish lineage and could often be found kilted, with Guinness-in-hand, among a group of City-Jocks at Ireland v Scotland rugby internationals in Dublin. He was one of our star research analysts and was also a star joker, causing much merriment when he telephoned another colleague, replete with a fake American drawl, pretending to be a Merrill compliance officer.

'Is that Pete Deighton,' the voice on the telephone said. 'Yes, how can I help?'

'This is Bret Wurlitzer, Head of Compliance, Merrill Lynch, Europe, Middle East and Africa,' came the careful but stern reply. 'You mentioned the word Apache at today's morning meeting. Do you know that that's a derogatory term for a race of Native American people?'

Pete was a walking encyclopaedia of information relating to the development pipeline of US and European aircraft and engine manufacturers like Airbus, Boeing, McDonald Douglas, and Rolls Royce. For several years prior to its 1997 launch, he had referred to Boeing's helicopter in code terms, AH-64. But on that morning, he spoke of the Apache Helicopter, to which the UK's Rolls Royce was supplying engines.

'Oh, I'm sorry, I didn't mean to cause offence,' said Pete, who was always a gentleman.

'I understand, it was a mistake,' said Bret, 'but please don't use that derogatory word again. You must call it the Native American Indian helicopter.'

It was not long before Pete was overheard to use the word Apache on a call to the investment team at Royal & Sun Alliance, and the call came again from Bret Wurlitzer.

'Mr Deighton, we have put a trace on your phone calls, and we have just heard you use that word in a call with Royal and Sun and Alliance. If it happens again you will be fired!'

'Deighton's not allowed to use the word Apache,' said a sales colleague when I returned from lunch.

'Not allowed to do what?' I replied quizzically. But we

would not have long to wait to see how Pete would react on the dealing room squawk box, as he was due to speak at the 2.30pm afternoon meeting.

'The AH-64..' Pete began to gasps around the dealing room. Two years after SNC had become part of the behemoth, one sales colleague could countenance no more interference from the Merrill Compliance Department and marched straight off to confront a bemused Brad. It was not long before he was made to look very foolish indeed.

By the time that colleague returned to his desk there was uproar around the dealing room, as the call from Bret Wurlitzer had been revealed to be a hoax by Tam MacStair!

In the summer of 1999, Merrill led the IPO of Eircom, Ireland's first big TMT opportunity, along with the Dublin-arm of the Dutch bank ABN Amro, and Ireland's AIB Goodbody.

Prior to listing as Eircom, Telecom Éireann the Irish state telecom company, was regarded as a boring utility with steady but unspectacular growth prospects, as well as a large capital expenditure requirement that would eat into future revenues that might otherwise be distributed to shareholders.

Now, rapid growth at its cellular telephony subsidiary, Eircell, elevated it into a new league of TMT stocks, along with global titans like Vodafone.

The IPO was launched just nine-months before the bursting of the dotcom bubble. AIB Goodbody was handling the share allocation to Irish investment institutions, so as the float approached, I was busy arranging the Omagh Fund Derby weekend fundraiser, awaiting the Eircom pricing announcement.

I had been excluded from the inter-broker discussions where the key question was how to value the offer in the face of unprecedented, tech-fuelled, demand.

Encouraged by an Irish Government campaign of wider

share ownership, it was speculated that up to 500,000 private clients would seek to buy shares.

Having made money stagging UK privatisations nearly twenty years before, I cautioned my investment bank colleagues, in the days prior to listing, not to overprice the issue. My overture was not well received, and my concerns fell on deaf ears.

Eircom's Employee Shareholder Trust (ESOT) had been allocated one-third of the shares before the IPO, and strong demand from Irish investment institutions meant that 80% of the stock would be placed with them and the ESOT.

It was clear that Eircom was set for a positive start to trading and I encouraged one of my blue-chip City clients to seek shares in the pre-trade book-build. Having been issued at €3.90 the indicative pre-market price from our overnight orderbook was nearly €5, a 25% gain.

'What shall we do with our 2m shares in Eircom?' said my client before the start of official trading. They were viewed as a 'long-term' investor and the allocation far-exceeded their expectations, or mine.

'That's a big profit. I'd sell.' I said.

'Sell how many?'

'Sell them all,' I replied.

To the dismay of Brad and many Merrill colleagues, the sale of all 2m shares just before the opening bell of the stock market killed the buying momentum that came from Merrill's US and Asian clients, and the shares promptly fell on the 8am market open, causing losses for many of our clients, and a €2m overnight profit for mine.

Eircom never saw the €5 pre-market price again, and within a year was 50% lower. Within two years it had sold Eircell at a 'knock-down' price to Vodafone and months later, at the end of 2001, was taken private and delisted by a consortium led by Goldman Sachs and Tony O'Reilly, at a third of the €3.90 IPO price.

Irish fund managers had successfully ridden the TMT wave by investing in European telecom stocks, and mobile handset manufacturers. But now, as well as owning half of Eircom, they had big positions in Vodafone and Germany's Mannesmann AG, just as the TMT bubble was about to burst.

Vodafone temporarily came to the rescue by launching a hostile bid for the giant Mannesmann. It was then the biggest corporate takeover offer ever, worth $120 billion.

Such was the size of the stake in Vodafone held by Irish institutions, that Sir Julian Horne Smith, Deputy Chief Executive, visited Dublin with me after every set of annual results. But on this occasion, we were defending Mannesmann, whose management was determined to rebut the aggressive suitor.

Merrill's bankers did an excellent job advising Mannesmann, and when the deal was completed in February 2000, three-months after the contest began, Vodafone agreed to pay 50% more than the first offer; $180 billion.

At $350 billion, the combined group was now the fourth largest company in the world after Microsoft, GE and Cisco.

The dotcom bubble finally burst in March 2000, one month after the deal concluded. Over the next three years, more than two-thirds of the merged group's market value was wiped out, making the combined group worth significantly less than Vodafone had paid for Mannesmann.

I had generated huge revenues selling shares in both companies before the deal completed as fund managers scrambled to reduce their exposure to telecom stocks, and my Irish client revenues soared from $16m in 1999 to $28m in 2000, a figure largely maintained in 2001 despite substantially lower share prices, as global stock markets continued to collapse.

I had now secured the two nominations from existing Merrill Managing Directors that were necessary to seek to join the top 5% of our 66,000 staff. But when I filled out the Managing Director Candidate Self-Evaluation form, I feared that the balance of argument would be skewed against me.

The message from my annual peer review continued a theme that had been developing since 1996. *Not a team player.*

Peer reviews were based on the Merrill Lynch Principles, a set of standards championed by Dan Tully that sought to define the shared values within our ever-expanding firm.

Those foundations were literally set in stone in the foyer of our St Paul's headquarters, as they were engraved in the marble panels that adorned the reception area through which 6,000 people entered every day. On that wall, the Principles read like a biblical script:

Merrill Lynch Principles:
Client Focus
Respect for the Individual
Teamwork
Responsible citizenship
Integrity

Positive peer review comments such as 'a first-class salesman and a very strong team player' were perplexingly juxtaposed with the words, 'not a team player.'

I blamed jealous colleagues, or 'incumbents', a term I used to describe those whom I judged owed their success to their old school tie, and to the Merrill Lynch business card that they carried. Were they not incumbent in that St. Paul's seat, they would never have made it in The City.

When you called from Merrill Lynch, people listened.

As Relationship Manager, and later Country Manager, for Ireland, I arranged and attended meetings for New York-based Merrill Executives with Irish corporate and investment chiefs, Government officials, and the Prime Minister, Bertie Ahern.

None of my peers seemed especially keen to hear that I had lunched overlooking the Hudson River, gazing at the Statue of Liberty, with Irish Treasury executives, Dan Tully's successor,

Dave Komansky, and his heir apparent, Stan O'Neal, in Merrill's 34th floor boardroom, Four World Financial Center, Lower Manhattan.

When appointed Head of our huge US Private Client Group, Stan had taken steps to cull the Thundering Herd. A year later, 2002, O'Neal was named The Most Powerful Black Executive in America by Fortune Magazine. In time he would succeed Dave as Chairman and CEO. Stan was not at all like Dave, nor Dan, and was apparently hostile to the notion of Mother Merrill which he was said to regard as cronyism.

Instead he seemed intent on using Merrill's 'financial' capital rather than our 'people' capital, by cutting the headcount and gearing up the balance sheet, actions that many later blamed for Merrill's downfall following the 2008 Financial Crisis. By the time he resigned in 2007 with a $160m severance package, the firm had adopted huge risk positions in the US Subprime Mortgage market, along with Lehman Brothers and other global investment banks.

Following an amicable chat with Dave at one end of the huge forty-seat Boardroom table, I moved with the two Irish Treasury Executives to an adjacent office to meet with Stan who had recently been promoted to President of the firm. Many years before, Stan had met the more senior Treasury official at a meeting in Dublin and after some reminiscing about the 'old days' I attempted to steer the conversation towards the business of the day. In that moment Stan's eyes seemed to burn and I felt an imaginary knife pierce my chest. Shut up, underling, appeared to be the message, and I did.

I had already been wary of Stan, as a former SNC Executive had mistaken him for a Bloomberg repair engineer and uttered profanities about his lateness, before our leader introduced himself to the bearded colleague, who, despite being an SNC Director, left the firm a few months later. 'I'm not from Bloomberg, I'm your new Chief Financial officer,' said Stan.

But my meeting with the great and the good in New York seemed to cause an unspoken wrath from Brad and other King Edward Street colleagues, particularly when Dave subsequently stopped by my City desk to say hello.

In the words of one peer group assessor, I needed to 'be careful of being too political'.

I had nothing to prove.

I could point to a trophy list of copy dealing sheets that sat on my desk, reminders of huge trades being done by my clients; SELL 3.5m RBS (£38m); BUY 5m BATS (£30m); and BUY 2m WPP (£18m), the latter being part of a £100m purchase.

I had discussed Mergers and Acquisitions with Sir Chris Gent, Vodafone, (Mannesmann), Sir Richard Sykes, Glaxo Smithkline, (Wellcome Trust), Sir John Browne, BP, (Amoco), Sir Martin Sorrell WPP, (Young & Rubicam), and Fred Goodwin, RBS, (NATWEST), a target then three times the size of its suitor.

But despite the huge trades and fascinating insights from the captains of British Industry, I was contemplating leaving Merrill Lynch and The City.

I was bored.

I had been a devoted disciple of Dan and Mother Merrill and believed that the Principles reflected what Merrill was all about. But the Principles were being turned against me. I loved Mother Merrill but Mother Merrill no longer loved me.

'NEEDS TO BE MORE WILLING TO SHARE INFORMATION WITH HIS COLLEAGUES,' blasted a peer review. 'Keeps to himself—could do with more interaction with sales and research,' said another, and 'only looks after number one', read the first three comments under the heading Development Needs in my year-end 2000 peer evaluation.

Under the heading Strengths, another said: 'A PLEASURE TO DEAL WITH. KNOWS HIS CLIENTS WELL.'

Groupthink was poisoning common sense. Although I

scored excellent marks overall, and top grades in another measure from the peer review, Client Focus, I scored badly on Teamwork.

But I would wake at an ungodly hour and keep on doing it, morning noon and night. It was like a never-ending game of poker, with a need to win every time.

In its hubris, Merrill embarked on what it called *The War for Talent*, a message that we sought to hire the world's best investment professionals; yet seemed intent on alienating me.

'You were the best of them all,' said Michael P, many years later. He was the most senior sales colleague with whom I worked throughout my eleven years at SNC and Merrill. The words seemed greatly ironic since I had in fact been brought down by many of 'them all'.

CHAPTER TWENTY-THREE

Reconciliation

'What do you buy the man who has everything?' my sister Marie was wont to say at Christmas visits home.

I was now among the top 1% of all UK taxpayers, and was 'earning more than The Arsenal.'

By 2001, my work desk at the magnificent Merrill Lynch Financial Centre at St. Paul's was a long way from the table at the overnight café at the neighbouring Smithfield Meat Market, where I had sat twenty years before, fingering my rubbish GCSE results as we waited for a trailer load of beef.

Through Merrill I had lived the American Dream. I had not quite made it from the log cabin to the White House but had graduated from the stinking hovel above Kate's Bar to the marbled corridors of No. 2, King Edward Street, London.

The contrast between my life and that of my brother, Paul, could not have been greater. I had not spoken with him in the eight years since Paddy's death, as I raged at the thought of his name.

There was no sadness in that feeling, no remorse for the loss, just pure anger at all the things I judged he had done to me.

Then, baby Kate was born on May 8, 2001 at Queen Charlotte & Chelsea Hospital, to *Adagio for Strings*.

I didn't know how to react when a handwritten note arrived before her birth, followed afterwards by a home-computer-generated card with a picture of a rabbit on the front. Inside were words of delight about the birth of baby Kate. They were words from Paul.

Paul had struggled since the Christian Brothers kicked him out. He was fourteen then. He entered his first alcohol dependency unit, months after we left the TB Hospital, aged eighteen.

At the end of my first day of lectures at Queen's University, Belfast, in 1983, I visited him at another high dependency unit at nearby Shaftsbury Square. He was twenty-two.

Yet I had never given him any credit for turning it all around, for graduating with a Science degree through the Open University while working as a storeman, for getting married, for becoming a Chemistry teacher in Edinburgh, and for being sober for fourteen years.

I struggled to accept the goodwill. How could he simply breeze back into my life without remorse for the damage done?

Despite our 'have it all out' hospital conversation, when he'd replied calmly, 'I'm sorry, but I don't remember any of that', I was still angry with him.

I was also angry with Merrill having been blackballed in my quest to become a Managing Director. I was advised to apply again at the end of 2001. Brad said that I needed to be more 'supportive' of our corporate transactions and needed to try harder at being a 'team player'. I looked back at him with undisguised rage.

I was one of the biggest revenue generators in the Merrill Lynch Europe, Middle East, and Africa (EMEA) region, but was not a Managing Director, and given my large pay package relative to many of my knockers, developed a dark, unspoken, mantra for the incumbents, 'I'm Chris McGale, who the fuck are you?'

My antipathy to Brad was now rampant. I felt I was a far better stockbroker than he had ever been. He was capable, but it seemed to me that in being an archetypal Merrill executive, a tall man with a full head of his own hair, his ascent to management had perhaps more to do with stereotype than ability.

I hated Brad.

I was earning a million dollars a year but hated going to work.

Throughout the decade before, with SNC and Merrill, I had never met any City headhunter and always declined the opportunity to even talk on the telephone with another firm.

As the champagne flowed in the corporate box at Royal Ascot in June 2001, I listened intently as Andy Stewart, Chairman and co-founder of Collins Stewart Plc., extolled the virtues of his growing firm that had listed on the stock market a year before and was now worth £350m.

As I watched Rebel Rebel battle hard to win the Ascot Gold Cup, it seemed that Collins Stewart would work perfectly for me.

By the end of 2001, I had two nominations running in parallel, my second attempt to become a Merrill MD, and in recognition of my work for the Omagh Fund, a nomination in the 2002 New Year's Honours List.

I had decided not to pursue the Collins Stewart opportunity and instead to stay and fight again for the MD title. In a fractious exchange with Brad, I presented him with an ultimatum: 'Promote me or I leave.' I was determined not to leave without my MD 'trophy'.

To achieve the Royal award, I was required to prepare a resume of my work for the Omagh Fund and outline other charitable contributions I had made. That included a charity auction that I arranged on the London trading floor for the victims of the Mozambique floods of 2000, which had raised £30,000 for distribution through the Disasters Emergency Committee.

At the auction, I spent £2,000 on a donated case of six bottles of Château Pichon Longueville Comtesse de Lalande, 1985, an exquisite wine that would be safely stored for some future celebration.

I had never imagined being a nominee in the New Year's

Honours List, but I was hopeful of being included.

I knew that the 2001 Merrill Christmas Party, at Dublin's Four Seasons Hotel, would probably be my last. It was our biggest ever, and four hundred invited guests were seated in the dining room, when as Country Manager for Ireland, I introduced our guest of honour, Dan Tully, Chairman Emeritus, Merrill Lynch & Co. Inc.

The Taoiseach, Bertie Ahern, arrived after dinner to meet with Dan and described me 'as the guy who gets everything done'.

'He's a hustler, that's for sure,' said Dan, with a twinkle in his eye. Later that evening he tried in vain to convince me to stay at Merrill.

'What age are you now?'

'I'll be thirty-nine next week.'

'You know I didn't come down to New York until I was forty,' he said, referencing the start of an ascent that would lead him to the top of our 66,000-staff firm.

That morning, I had waited in the foyer of Dublin's Merrion Hotel for his arrival following an overnight flight from New York. There he had greeted the bellboys and reception staff like long-lost friends, as he would later the guests at the Christmas party.

A few weeks before I had brought another Merrill superstar, Henry Blodget, to meet with Dublin investor clients and Fran Rooney, Baltimore Technologies Plc., CEO.

Baltimore had been a major problem for me as I had not promoted it to my clients, much to the chagrin of investment banking colleagues, Brad, and the company's executives.

'You're a dinosaur, Chris,' said a junior work colleague with no little malice, referencing my non-participation in the Baltimore cheerleading.

A loss-making Irish company, it had listed on the LSE via the reverse takeover of a small 'shell' company, but its 'sexy' internet security technology enabled eCommerce, and its soaring share price facilitated two acquisitions for Baltimore with a combined value of more than $1 billion.

Its meteoric rise saw it listed among the UK's largest companies on two out of the four quarterly reviews the year before. It first entered the FTSE 100 index in March 2000, with a market value of £6 billion, ($9 billion) was demoted in June, having lost two-thirds of its value, and was reselected in September following another doubling of its share price.

Now, it was tumbling again.

Chinese walls protocol meant I could not attend the meeting between Blodget and Rooney, and was obliged to interrupt the over-running discourse so that Henry could proceed to meetings with our institutional investor clients.

At first, I popped my head into the meeting room, and light heartedly said that Merrill cutbacks meant that we had dispensed with a limo and had a taxi waiting outside with its meter running. Five minutes later I returned to say that the meter was still running, to which an irritated Fran replied, 'The next time I see you, Chris, you'll be driving the taxi!'

He was more right than he knew.

In the limo, Henry gave nothing away about his meeting. Being a New York-based analyst, he had never written a research comment on Baltimore and was reluctant to comment on its worth.

'How much cash is on its balance sheet?' he asked, after much gentle probing by me.

'About £90 million.'

'I guess it's worth £90 million then,' he said, cryptically, compared to its multi-billion-pound market value.

A year later, Rooney was gone, and Baltimore's value had declined by billions.

It was then in the 99% club, having lost all but 1% of its peak value less than eighteen months before. After $1 billion of Merrill-advised acquisitions, the company was delisted from the stock market, and returned its remaining £20m cash to shareholders.

As the New Year of 2002 came and went, Royal protocol meant that I was not contacted regarding the New Year's Honours List, having failed to be included on it.

I had, finally, been added to the Merrill elite and became Managing Director, Global Markets & Investment Banking. With our wives the MD graduates were invited to join executives for a celebratory dinner at a fine hotel on London's Strand. But I felt like a party gatecrasher and the ample champagne that flowed fell flat in my glass.

I no longer wished to be 'a team player'. I was still scoring the goals and winning big deals, but the crowds no longer cheered when I netted the big-money trades, and for the first time in 11 years, my Irish client revenues were down on the year before.

'Remember, you can make a difference,' I had written in the letter to potential guests at the Omagh fundraising lunch with Tony Blair, but when I attended a quarterly meeting of country managers in March 2002, I wondered what difference I was making.

Everyone around the table was a Managing Director, including some that had obstructed my promotion, and the subject matter at the meeting was graduate recruitment.

There I listened as a South African colleague suggested that the firm appeared to be hiring largely Oxford, Cambridge, and LSE graduates, which he believed limited our opportunities in the new graduate market.

Most of the attendees had been to the best private schools money could buy, an advantage that gave them the arrogance and sense of entitlement that I saw in the incumbents. The *Oxbridge-plus* strategy would give Merrill a 'better bang for our buck', they argued. In the future Merrill would employ people in their image, and not people like me.

Having listened to an eloquent counterargument in favour of wider recruitment from my Johannesburg colleague, I chose not to contribute to the debate. Despite my strong views about education and opportunity, I said nothing.

I was the guy from Omagh Tech, sharing the table with these expensively crafted Masters of the Universe, yet I ducked the debate, and was ashamed.

Had I got to the top of my mountain? Was I really a duck out of water?

They had already been bringing people into the business in their own likeness and I had been vocal in objecting to that. My complaint was that they were handing out summer internships to people wholly unsuited for the business, young people who would not subsequently be selected to join our sales team. Our job was to sell equity trading ideas to investment managers but many of the candidates had no selling skills whatsoever.

'Why don't you do it then?' said Brad after another complaint from me about a barren summer internship programme. Instead of commenting informally on the inadequacies of the prospective sales colleagues, I was now required to participate in the formal cross-evaluation of each candidate, as they moved on a weekly basis through Equity Sales, Equity Research, Investment Banking and Fixed Income, Currencies, and Commodities (FICC).

'NOT SUITED TO THIS INDUSTRY,' I had written in tramlines across the Summer Internship Evaluation Form that would then be passed to the department where the intern would spend their next week at Merrill.

'That is not what we want from you!' said Brad when I handed the form to him. The US-born MBA student had spent a week with me and was super-confident about the prospect of working in our industry.

'You are supposed to complete the individual boxes commenting on his various strengths and weaknesses,' said Brad.

'I cannot recommend this individual in any way, so my comment reflects his many weaknesses.' I was bugged by his sense of entitlement and guessed his dad knew someone in New York, as he was an American working for an American investment bank in London. But he had zero people skills.

'You were right about that candidate,' said Brad three weeks later. 'He got bad reviews everywhere and argued with me when I tried to let him down gently.'

But my work with the interns seemed like ancient history on that day. I felt like an outsider in a business where we would now hire more people in the likeness of my Boardroom colleagues, not me.

'It's never forever,' were wise words I recalled from Sir John Ritblat, Chairman, British Land, and I finally decided to leave Merrill during a weeklong holiday in Ireland with Niamh and our soon-to-be one-year-old Kate at her parent's Wexford farm.

On my arrival at King Edward Street, I called Paul Roy's office to find that he was in the US on business. Paul was now part of the firm's Global Executive Management team and I saw little of him.

I travelled to Dublin on business the following day and did not go to the office on Wednesday, May 1, 2002. Instead, I telephoned Paul's P.A. to ask her to let him know that I was leaving the firm to 'spend more time with my family'.

'My daughter will be one-year-old in a week and I rarely see her.'

The whirl of helicopter blades nearly drowned the sound of his voice when Paul called me later. 'You think you have problems?' he said, 'I've just arrived in Washington to meet Eliot Spitzer!'

Spitzer, the New York Attorney General, and the so-called

Sheriff of Wall Street, was pursuing Merrill, and Henry Blodget, following the dotcom collapse.

Henry left Merrill, and Wall Street, and later co-founded Business Insider (BI) newswire, where Amazon's Jeff Bezos was an early investor, while Spitzer's public career ended in resignation and disgrace.

BI was later sold for $450m, while Henry's best-known share tip, Amazon, became the world's most valuable company – and is currently valued at $1,600,000,000,000 ($1.6trn), one-hundred-and-sixty times more valuable than then.

'Everyone needs to take a step back at some point,' said Paul Roy, and advised that I should not resign, but take a six-month sabbatical.

In any event, we would have a chance to discuss my plans three days later when I was Paul's guest at Newmarket, where his wife Sue's horse, Twilight Blues, was due to run in the 2000 Guineas race.

I had an interest in the race, as I had bet £10,000 on it.

The one-mile, or eight-furlong, 2000 Guineas is the first of the 'classic' races to be run in the UK horseracing calendar, and Irish trainer Aidan O'Brien had two of the fancied runners in the twenty-runner race: the even money (1/1) favourite, Hawk Wing, and the 10/1 third favourite, Rock of Gibraltar, (The Rock), who was partly owned by Sir Alex Ferguson.

As Merrill were corporate advisors to Man United, I had recently hosted investor meetings in Dublin for Peter Kenyon, CEO, and David Gill, CFO, Manchester United Plc.

John Magnier and JP McManus, already legendary for their roles as Ireland's most successful racehorse breeder, and gambler, respectively, three years later banked a profit of €125m on their €210m investment in Man Utd, when in 2005 they sold their near 30% stake in the club.

Magnier had gifted a stake in The Rock to Ferguson, an act of generosity that would later see the two men contest a legal action over that ownership.

To my mind the betting market had mispriced the 2000 Guineas race, as the Rock had beaten the Hawk over six furlongs in Ireland a year before, and subsequently won the principal form-line to the race, Newmarket's seven-furlong Dewhurst Stakes. For both races, The Rock had been a short-priced favourite.

As a parting gift to my Merrill colleagues, I told everyone who would listen on my final day at King Edward Street to bet on Rock of Gibraltar at 10/1.

My bet was £5,000 each way.

Before the race, Niamh and I stood with Paul and Sue, Sir Alex, John Magnier, and others in the Newmarket Parade Ring, observing the expensively crafted horseflesh that passed.

Hawk Wing was a magnificent specimen, big and powerfully muscled, and made The Rock look slight by comparison. For the first time that week, I had doubts about his winning chance.

When the racing gates opened and one minute and thirty-seven seconds had elapsed, the two horses crossed the finish line separated by only a neck, and The Rock had begun a series of wins that would see him crowned European Horse of the Year (2002).

I had won £62,500.

The Rock won again five weeks later at Royal Ascot, when Andy Stewart once more encouraged me to meet with his colleague, Terry Smith. At lunch with Terry soon after, he told me of certain traits he looked for in prospective hires.

They included divorced or deceased parents and the death of a sibling. I ticked most of the boxes and could add a trait unique to me, a near-death experience. He was seeking people that had an innate hunger to succeed.

By the time I had made it from The City back to my West London home, an email had arrived containing an offer from

Terry. It was a *golden hello* contract that would potentially allow me to own 1% of Collins Stewart, worth £3.5 million, ($5m), subject to me achieving 50% of the business that I did annually for Merrill in Ireland.

But I had just got off The City treadmill, and I politely asked Terry for a few weeks to consider.

Niamh, Kate, and I now spent much of our time at a new Algarve villa that I had bought for €500,000 on the last day of our holiday there the year before.

A short time later, just weeks into my six-month leave of absence, I saw press reports about redundancies at Merrill and asked to be included. After eleven years of total commitment I accepted a six-figure voluntary redundancy package.

One third of my million-dollar 'compensation package' was made up of Merrill shares, and by way of 'deferred compensation', stock options. The value of both was disappearing fast in the dotcom malaise.

My income for the next three years would go to virtually zero, but I had my book to write.

I had burnt out and left Merrill in a blaze of rage, with no glory, and torched every hand that sought to offer me a bridge back.

The fight was over.

With my divorce from Merrill complete, and much-needed rest and recuperation planned for both Niamh and me, I returned to Collins Stewart to discuss their offer; but it had lapsed.

'I don't offer 1% of my company to just anyone,' said Terry.

By poetic justice, it was July 4, 2002– Independence Day.

I had planned to use any Dundalk car crash compensation to invest in pubs in Dublin. In 1991, that would almost certainly have proved to be a sterling investment, and given my propensity for risk, I would no doubt have graduated to the world of serious property development, with lots of development risk, and lots of bank debt. I would then, no doubt, have gone the way of many Irish developers, into the arms of Ireland's *bad bank*, the National Asset Management Agency (NAMA), and personal bankruptcy.

After the 2008 financial crisis, €64bn of the mortgage and development debt of Anglo Irish Bank, AIB Bank, Bank of Ireland, and others, was adopted by the State owned NAMA. As Ireland's Country Manager, I had met in an ambassadorial role a few of Anglo's *C-Suite* executives as Merrill advised them on debt securitisation, where packages of apparently high-quality mortgage debt were sold to international investors, thus freeing up funds for more lending to the booming Irish housing market.

By the time I met a senior Anglo private banker in the summer of 2002, a decade into the housing boom, I judged that I was too late to the party, but my Merrill CV gave me a significant leg-up with the banker who, keen to impress, opened a drawer to his right hand and flashed an imaginary pile of sales contracts for Dublin apartments, each said to be worth at least €25,000, any of which I could have. 'We can send over €30,000 if you need to buy a bit of jewellery for your wife,' he followed. I declined both offers.

I returned to The City three years later, for a short time with Andy Stewart at Cenkos Securities, a start-up firm named after one of his racehorses, where the small-cap and mid-cap focus didn't suit my large-cap FTSE knowledge base.

I then joined Numis Securities, a fabulous group of old-City professionals where I was ribbed about my constant references to Merrill.

A colleague rib-tickled me about my many Merrill triumphs. 'You're a legend, Chris,' he said with a smile and soon I developed another nickname, the Ledge.

I had left Merrill, but Merrill never left me.

Before Numis, in early 2005, I had talks with JP Morgan Chase & Co. Inc. who had indicated a 'signing-on' fee of $250,000, and a pre-bonus salary of $250,000 a year paid offshore in Jersey, but after a peer interviewer suggested to me that I might not be a team player, they made the offer conditional on the support of a specific Dublin institution. The relevant fund manager, who got the job in Dublin through my introduction, declined the offer to establish relations with JP Morgan, and no job offer was made to me.

Bulge-bracket investment banks no longer saw the need to have their 'man in Ireland,' as my Irish clients had suffered large outflows of funds under management after the dotcom crash when Eircom was delisted and Baltimore had gone bust, and telecom stocks like Vodafone then massively underperformed resurgent US tech stocks. Five years after the dotcom crash began in March 2000, the NASDAQ Index was now 80% higher than its 2002 low.

One of my last institutional client meetings with Merrill in Dublin was with Charles, Chip, Goodyear, BHB Billiton Plc., Chief Development Officer, an Ivy League American scion of the Goodyear family, who oozed class and perfect manners. It was only after the second of our springtime visits to Dublin that several investors bought into the company. Three years later BHP had doubled, and I hoped to leverage that success on my return to work in the City in 2005.

'We love you Chris, but without Merrill Lynch you're just another broker with a view,' said a Dublin-based, Italian fund manager at a US-owned, fund management group. He had given me a short window to prove my worth at Numis.

It seemed that I too had been a Merrill incumbent.

Without clients in The City you have nothing, and having lost my entire Irish client base, I saw an opportunity to target Prop Traders, a group of very smart investors who traded the 'proprietary' capital of global banks; as opposed to fund managers who managed funds on behalf of external clients.

Prop Traders bought or sold the news, whatever that may be – corporate announcements, IPO's, M&A – and did so large, fast, and often.

At Numis, two such clients became a great source of revenues for me, but I needed access to more FTSE, large-cap, research ideas to feed these deal-hungry traders.

Within a year I was headhunted to work for COC Securities, who had hired a team of analysts, sales traders, and market makers from some of The City's biggest firms.

It seemed to me that many of the sales team had not 'played at the highest level' and, as a sweetener to encourage me to join, I was offered an opportunity to 'graduate' to the Head of Sales role. I had never sought the position at Merril and didn't particularly want it at COC either.

I met the incumbent HoS at my last interview with the firm and understood that he was aligned with the plan. He had not worked for a bulge-bracket firm and, naively, I presumed that in time he would be happy to pass the mantle to me.

And so, at the end of my first working day, in time-honoured City tradition, I made my way to a nearby hostelry with the HoS, and we were soon joined there by his Deputy HoS, whom I had not met nor heard of, who had arrived straight from a boozy lunch.

When our host went to the bar to get him another drink, the happy Deputy HoS asked me about my clients, and I explained my plan to target Prop Traders. Pressing me further about my largest fee generators, I named one of the two bank clients and felt the trapdoor open beneath me

In the blink of an eye he reached for his mobile phone, called my client and said the following: 'Gavin, I'm here with Chris McGale – he says that he is your highest paid broker – you wee bastard, you always told me that I was!'

I had been ambushed and my client relationship was

destroyed. It was the end of my first day at the firm, and the beginning of the end of my career at COC.

In the weeks that followed, I managed the mutual hostility with the sidekick by imagining him as the *Austin Powers, Goldmember* character, Fat Bastard.

Hello, Fat Bastard, I said in my head as I approached the ground floor elevator at our City office late one afternoon but did not utter a word. I presumed that he was waiting for our boss after a boozy lunch, and a nod and fake smile were all I offered.

'My cock in your mouth,' he sneered in a nasty Scottish accent, leaning down on me, stinking of alcohol. I continued into the lift and smiled at my reflected image in the elevator. No bully drunk was going to get the better of me.

When, a few weeks later, I was called before the Chief Executive, Head of Human Resources, Head of Legal, and Head of Sales to have my contract terminated after only five months, I relayed the story to an aghast group.

'If you don't believe me ask him,' I said, pointing to the nodding Head of Sales to whom I had reported the incident. They had offered to pay me a six-figure sum to leave, and I didn't seek any additional compensation, only a commitment that he would be reprimanded and that the incident would be reported to the Financial Services Authority.

One month later I joined another City firm in another six-figure deal, and the Fat Bastard continued at COC Securities.

More than ten years had passed since I last saw my brother Paul at Paddy's funeral, when I secured match tickets for him, his wife Jane, and other McGale family members, to attend the 2003 All Ireland Football Final in Dublin, when Tyrone would seek our first 32-county success against defending champions Armagh.

After his kind words on her birth, I had invited him to attend Kate's christening in London two years earlier, but he didn't make it.

We had been through so much pain in our lives, as children and as young adults; pain the birth of Kate, and then Joseph, had helped me move beyond. I wondered if parenthood would help heal Paul too.

President McAleese and Bertie Ahern, whose Honorary Doctor of Laws degree award ceremony I had attended as Dan Tully's guest just three days before at Fairfield University, Connecticut, stood behind the Tyrone Captain Peter Canavan as he lifted the Sam Maguire Cup following victory over Armagh.

It was the first time two Ulster teams contested the final, and as Bertie had predicted a few days before at Fairfield, the adjoining counties had a titanic struggle. For Paul and me, brother to brother, the outcome was so long in coming that we cried tears of joy.

But when I drove along John Street in a hire car two summers later, the evening before a family wedding, I saw him enter a pub and followed him onto the premises.

'Do you want a beer?' he said, amicably.

'Yes, I'll have the same as you,' I replied to my brother who had been sober for eighteen years.

It felt weird that none of the young bar staff knew who we were; the McGale's of John St! Otherwise it all felt normal. I was having a quiet beer with this super-fit, besuited, rational, schoolteacher, who despite the beer in hand, appeared once again to be *as sober as a judge*.

It's not for me to say,' I said once settled on the high stool, 'but what's the story? Are you drinking again?'

'Just a few beers,' he said.

'There was one thing I wanted to ask you,' he said later, after a bit of small talk.

'What's that?' I replied.

'Will you be my next of kin?' I then learned that he had split from his wife, who had nursed him nearly two decades before at Derry's Northlands Addiction Treatment Centre.

Later that year Paul sent a text message: 'HELP ME.' I travelled to Leith, Edinburgh. He opened the door of his Mitchell Street apartment and disappeared in his underwear to the front room.

I looked into the kitchen and saw maybe twenty empty clear-glass vodka bottles stacked neatly on a kitchen table. Partially covered by a blanket, I could see the fabulous physique of a marathon runner lying face down on a camp bed, and recalled the words of an Omagh running coach who described my then teenage sprinter brother to me as 'the one that got away'.

We travelled back to Omagh the following morning and our sisters gave him a bed at their homes, before he returned to Edinburgh and the drink.

The police contacted me in November 2005 to say that he had fallen heavily and was on a ventilator at the Western General Hospital, Edinburgh.

An epileptic due to alcohol abuse, he had fallen backwards, like a plank, and smashed the back of his skull causing multiple fractures and brain damage.

When I saw him a day later, a spike stuck out of the top of his head, as surgeons sought to relieve the pressure on his brain.

I held his hand and said, 'It'll be alright; it'll be alright.'

After a month-long coma, Paul spent another four months as a rehab inpatient at the Head Injury Unit of Edinburgh's Astley Ainslie Hospital having suffered near-total memory loss.

He had forgotten that he was a chemistry teacher at St David's High School, Dalkeith. His best friend, Noel, a Derryman who had moved in next door at Bonnyrigg, Midlothian, told me that he had begun his career at Scottish sink schools, where he sought to help disadvantaged primary school kids, and that he never worried about financial reward. Now he couldn't recognise the Periodic Table, but he always knew me.

'What's that song about Derry?' He asked, and I wondered whether he was remembering Northlands Hospital where he met Jane, a nurse at the alcoholic treatment centre, or whether he remembered the pain of the song; *The Town I Loved So Well*.

He had forgotten that he was a marathon runner, until he found medals from races he had run in.

He was helped enormously by Edinburgh's Headway Group, a brain-injury charity, and became a minor celebrity in January 2007, when BBC Scotland News reported his plans to raise funds for Headway by taking part in Edinburgh's Great Winter Run; under the news heading *Memory man to attempt uphill race*.

He was delighted to be given another chance for life and told the BBC that he was 'very lucky to be having a go at all, there are so many less fortunate than me. I'm just delighted to be alive and to be given another chance.' The news report included a video of him running around the grounds of Astley Ainslie Hospital, his head injury causing one side of his body to be out of sync with the other. My head injury does the same to my left side when I'm exposed to the cold.

I saw Paul in Omagh at Easter, a few months after the Edinburgh run. He was staying with Noelle, was in a good place mentally, and was happy.

Prior to my return to London, on Good Friday, April 6, 2007, we met up with Noelle, and Joanie at the former Kate's

Bar, in which I had invested £500,000 a year before, and where Joanie was now the manager.

I observed that the last time we had stood there on a Good Friday was nearly thirty years before, when we set off to the Forster Green TB hospital.

'I'm not sure,' said Paul, as he struggled with the memory,

At that moment, an elder cousin Kieran and his wife Anne walked past the pub, and to break the awkward impasse, I almost dragged them in from the street.

'What about Celtic?!' was the first thing Glasgow-born Kieran said, to which Paul recounted a story about watching indifferently a Celtic v. Rangers match with patients at Astley Ainslie, before he began to remember that he was a Celtic fan. In fact, he was a fanatical, season-ticket-holding Celtic fan.

He had also forgotten that he was a chronic alcoholic and never drank again.

Kieran had lived above the pub as a child following his family's return to Omagh, a discussion that prompted Paul to tell a story about our father dog-whistling up the yard at the back of the pub to attract his brother Arthur's attention to a furniture-business call received on the pub's 364 telephone number; the then three-hundred-and-sixty-fourth phone number in Omagh.

It was the first time I had heard that story.

He spoke enthusiastically about having restarted basic chemistry lessons and how he hoped one-day to return to teaching.

He had come a long way.

I called him three months later to offer my debenture seats at Croke Park for the Tyrone v Meath All Ireland Quarter Final in early August, 2007, four years after our first All-Ireland triumph, and two years after our second.

I offered to take care of everything, his flights and accommodation, and for a mutual friend to meet-and-greet him at Dublin Airport, but as I wouldn't be there, he declined.

So, I promised to meet with him in Dublin for the Semi Final two weeks later.

Tyrone didn't make it, nor did Paul.

It was the last time we talked.

The uphill race proved to be more than a metaphor, and he died of a brain haemorrhage, sober and alone in his Leith flat on August 31, 2007.

We had all been on holiday, but I knew the morning that Noelle called to ask if I had heard from him that he was dead.

On the day Paul's body was found, I had arranged a midweek business lunch at 1 Lombard Street, a fine restaurant beside Bank Station in the City. I had booked the lunch venue weeks in advance, intending to impress my guest whom I had not met before, but spent much of that morning juggling work calls with my sisters and the Edinburgh Police.

Not long after I departed for the 1pm lunch meeting, Constable McFarland called to say that he was outside the Mitchell Street flat but could not gain access. Then from the steps of the restaurant, I called Paul's friend Noel who held spare keys and told him that I feared Paul was dead. He had not heard from Paul either.

'I'm sorry,' I said almost as soon as my guest and I had sat down. 'I should really have cancelled our meeting. I have been exchanging calls for the past few hours with the police in Edinburgh. They will soon get access to my brother's flat. He might be dead.'

Our worst fears were confirmed halfway through lunch.

We took Paul home to Tyrone via road and ferry, with a local undertaker transferring his body at Belfast Harbour to an Omagh funeral director. I flew from London that morning and arrived at the port to find my sisters, Jane, and Noel, whom I had not met, awaiting the body.

As I approached the group on the outdoor terminal, as disembarking lorries drove by, a young lady stepped forward to embrace me, and I didn't recognise her. It was Ciara, Noelle's eldest, who had been like an eighth McGale at John Street, when Briegie, Joanie, and I were at school, and later at Church Hill with her beloved Granda, Paddy.

My head was frazzled, but I drove to Omagh with Noel as my passenger where for the next one-and-a-half hours we exchanged stories of Paul's forty-six-years; me relating to the first half of his life and Noel to the last decade.

At the Omagh morgue, my sisters and Jane stayed with the closed coffin. I looked in from an adjacent room and became aware of the sound of something tapping persistently on a steel door. As people looked my way, I realised that the heel of my hyperactive left foot was causing the vibration.

He was then taken to the Sacred Heart Church and that evening I worked on a partly-drafted eulogy that started with the words, 'If you Google Paul McGale.' The first name I came across was a medical statistician at the University of Oxford, and I mused how that in a different world, that could have been my brother. He was buried in the family plot with Mum, Dad, Martin, and Paddy.

Paul's death devastated me.

I had conditioned myself to believe that grief was a form of self-pity, but the bereavement broke my defences and broke my heart, bringing to the fore all the deaths that had gone before.

I survived and everyone else died.

Catharsis was my objective when I left The City and began writing eighteen years ago. Niamh and I have been married for twenty-two-years. Baby Kate is now nineteen, Joseph seventeen and Alice fifteen. It is my story about the death of a family, Mum, Dad, and Martin, and my own near-death.

Paul hardly got a mention in my early drafts. I hated him. Then I learned to love him, again.

'Give me a hug brother,' he said, when I saw him at Kate's Bar for the last time.

I had been delighted to do just that.

Six months later, on March 7, 2008, one day before Mum's thirty-third anniversary, Thomas Paul McGale was born in London.

CHAPTER TWENTY-FOUR

Losing My Religion

Apollo 11 landed on the Moon in 1969, when I was six, and Paul told me that we were related to Commander Neil Armstrong, the first man to walk on the Moon. We had cousins in America, but Paul's Moon-landing cousin claim was a dream too far.

Paul told me about the great Irish racehorse trainer Vincent O'Brien, who trained Nijinsky to win the 1970 Epsom and Irish Sweepstake Derbies. Paul said he was the greatest racehorse ever. The Irish Derby was held at the Curragh Racecourse and we learned the words of The Curragh of Kildare, a much-aired ballad where *small birds* were said to be *singing in the trees*. Paul said it was sung by our 'cousin,' Paul Brady.

Paul followed the early career of a young tennis player from Cork, Sean Sorensen, whom he said was the cousin of the family of a local doctor. He would later play at Wimbledon in 1977, the first Irishman to qualify for the main draw of a tennis Grand Slam.

Paul said we would support Ireland playing Tiddlywinks, we would support Ireland in every game, in every way. We cheered Ulster's Willie John McBride and Mike Gibson in Ireland's rugby team but by the time of Paul's death my love for gambling had trumped my loyalty to Irish teams.

Prior to my sabbatical from Merrill in 2002, Handicap Betting on international Rugby Union games, where draws are rare, were my favourite place to bet big. I sat in an Executive Box at the Stade de France with Merrill clients exhibiting faux disappointment as the Fabien Galthié-led hosts hammered Ireland 43-5. I had bet £12,000 on France, minus ten points, for a win of £10,000.

It was a soulless, joyless, triumph made worse as Niamh and I had travelled to and from Paris with London-Irish friends who were initially optimistic and then deflated by the outcome. Soon after I closed all my gambling accounts and quit betting on horses and sport. Instead, I put all my energies into writing my memoir and maintained that self-imposed betting abstinence for the next three years. My betting vows were tested when I saw odds of 7/1 offered against the media-friendly Cardinal Ratzinger to become Pope; but my vows were tested, not broken.

My desire to gamble was driven by a desire to win, and I always had a strategy. I had declined the honeymoon visit to Las Vegas and had no interest in playing against *the house* at a casino or trying to outsmart a gaming machine. As my days at Merrill came to an end, my gambling on horses became instinctive rather than studied, and for the first time I was losing. It was time to quit.

Fortunately, like poker, there was an easy way to give up. Don't attend the game, or in the case of horseracing don't go to the track and don't read the racing pages. Racehorses have a short shelf life, so it was easy to become unfamiliar with the names of the new breed of thoroughbred champions, until in time they represented no interest at all.

At the 1995 Rugby World Cup in South Africa, seven years before, I had bet £8,000 on New Zealand at pre-tournament odds of 15/8 and was counting the money before the Final against hosts South Africa, when the All-Blacks' odds were now super-short at 1/4. But the disappointment felt by the surprise win of the underdog hosts was quickly tempered by the sight of Nelson Mandela, President of South Africa, presenting the Webb Ellis Cup to his Captain, Francois Pienaar, while wearing a Springboks' rugby shirt and cap. Six years later, in 2001, while Niamh was pregnant with our firstborn Kate, we stood inside the Robben Island cell in which Mandela had spent much of his twenty-seven-years in captivity.

'Jonah Lomu to be top try scorer,' said the unsuspecting former England Coach, Dick Best, when I asked at a Merrill client event for his surprise outcome at the forthcoming 1999 Rugby World Cup. Lomu had burst onto the stage four years earlier, when joint top-scorer with seven tries in the 1995 World Cup, including two against Ireland in the opening round and four against England in the semi-final.

In the meantime, he had been diagnosed with a serious kidney disorder and did not start, nor score, in any of New Zealand's four Tri Nations Series matches earlier in the World Cup year. At the 16/1 being offered by oddsmakers, I was reminded of the adage I'd learned many years before, 'the horse doesn't know what price it is.' Jonah scored five tries in the opening three matches and eight in all, even though the All-Blacks lost the semi-final to France, and I won £16,000.

'I have a betting strategy for the Rugby World Cup,' I said to Niamh, before the start of the 2007 competition, where New Zealand were red-hot favourites. But the value bet appeared to be South Africa at odds of 8/1. As those teams were on different sides of the fixture matrix my strategy was to bet on them both, with an All-Black win being a 'hedge' that would result in a small financial gain, and a Springbok win producing a big result.

The bet was £5,000 on South Africa to win the tournament

'without New Zealand' at 1/1 and another £5,000 on South Africa to win it outright at 8/1. The hedge meant that if both teams met in the final, I couldn't lose. I also put £2,000 on Bryan Habana to be top try scorer at odds of 7/2. When South Africa were triumphant, the £12,000 staked resulted in a net win of £52,000.

With World Cup games coming around every week, and with impact injuries sustained during an eighty-minute rugby international considered equivalent to those of a car crash, I judged that the top teams would seek to protect their best players, and embarked on another strategy for the tournament - bet the underdog with a big handicap points start. In the opening game I backed Argentina +12 points to beat France before they shocked the host nation with a 5-point win at the 80,000-seat Stade de France.

Ireland would be my whipping boys of the tournament. My head would rule my heart. They were ranked what I thought to be an unjustified fifth in the world, ahead of England, Wales, and Argentina, and would play the latter in Group D along with France, Georgia, and Namibia. In handicap bets, I bet against Ireland in every game winning a further £25,000. That added to a net five positive results from other matches at 10/11, meant I had won a tax-free total of £100,000.

'I need the money, I have a lot going on,' I said ruefully to a surprised Irish buddy who joined me in a quiet London wine bar where we could cheer South Africa against England, the defending champions. I would make £200,000 in the City that year, including a £100,000 bonus, and had been negotiating to sell Kates Bar where the bidding had started at £1.5m and I had declined an offer of £2.01m. The prospective buyer was one of three bidders and had offered £2m but I asked for £2.1m and negotiations ended.

I then agreed to retain a one-third stake in a consortium that included Tyrone's All-Ireland winning captain from four years before, Peter Canavan. That deal valued the premises at £2m and the funding was agreed with AIB Bank, but I decided to go-it-alone and withdrew the sale. Not long after, the first bidder, a nightclub owner, had stood respectfully outside his premises diagonally opposite the old Kate's Bar on John Street Corner as we followed Paul's hearse.

'I'm in the assets game,' I had said when stalling the planned pub sale, emphasising that I was trading properties to add value and sell them again. I wasn't so concerned about the income the pub might generate, as due to my City salary, it would be taxed at the 40% Higher Rate tax band.

Between 2006 and 2008, I had spent £650,000 upgrading the pub, and acquired after a competitive bidding process for £300,000 the grocery store that now acted as a gateway to the development properties at the rear of the pub. I had sold it twenty years before for £25,000.

In 2007 I paid €180,000 in cash as a 20% deposit on a €900,000 Algarve villa. The villa I bought in 2002 for €500,000 was also now valued at €900,000. In the same year I had spent £500,000 on a buy-to-let apartment in West London.

I had a property inheritance for each of our four children, and a diversified portfolio, I thought. But I had ignored the wise counsel I had given myself when Anglo Irish Bank offered me an open chequebook half-a-dozen years before. My empire had been built on debt – and it was the biggest gamble of my life, even if I didn't see it that way. And then it all went wrong.

Lehman Brothers filed for bankruptcy and the 2008 Financial Crisis erupted.

After Lehman, Merrill Lynch was bailed-out by Bank of America, rendering my once-million-dollar options worthless, my £2m pub was now unsellable in a frozen Irish property market, and a decade would pass before it was sold for

£570,000; 70% or £1.44m less than I had declined for it. In that same year, 2018, I finally exited the Portuguese properties and the London buy-to-let apartment for small profits.

'I had a near-death experience,' a former City client said when I met him on the street in Dublin, a year-and-a-half after Lehman. He was referring to the prospect of his stock portfolio being decimated, before global central banks pushed interest rates sharply lower, and Wall Street was now once again in the ascendency.

'If you only knew,' I mumbled as I smiled to myself and ambled off in the other direction. By his criteria I had been through a second near-death experience, but my fate was much worse than he could begin to understand.

Two years later, and more than three after the so-called *Great Recession* began, I was back in Dublin meeting officials from the Irish Treasury's National Pension Reserve Fund (NPRF).

'I have a great idea,' I explained to two executives that I had known for many years. My proposal was to find a UK Private Equity business partner that would contribute equal funds on a joint-venture basis with the NPRF in a fund worth €100m. The fund would provide much-needed investment capital to Ireland's ailing Small & Medium Enterprise (SME) sector.

The partner I had in mind was Better Capital Plc, with whose founder, Jon Moulton, I travelled to Dublin two months later, in February 2012.

As London's *Evening Standard* newspaper reported in 2015, I had shaken hands with Moulton after the NPRF meeting, to confirm terms I had presented to him by email the evening before, prior to a meeting with him at his office.

Shortly afterwards I learned with great surprise from Moulton's colleague that they would not be proceeding with the proposed collaboration.

I nearly dropped the newssheet onto the lap of a London

Underground commuter when I read a year later that the two parties had launched a €100m SME/Turnaround Fund.

As the *Evening Standard* reported, Moulton countered that he did an altogether different deal with Treasury officials, whom Better Capital met in London less than two weeks after he travelled to Dublin with me. Moreover, the alternative route to the deal suggested that Better Capital were introduced by the Dublin head of a Bahamas-based law firm.

To paraphrase what I wrote later in a letter to the Taoiseach, Enda Kenny, after the fund was shut down; 'It is remarkable that a Turnaround Fund set up for the benefit of Irish SMEs, would operate for two years and not find a single opportunity in which to invest; a huge disaster for Irish SMEs. Was that because of the hullabaloo I caused by raising the fee dispute?'

'Let's shake hands on that €1m fee,' I had said to Moulton, offering my right hand in a taxi on our way to Dublin Airport, and we did.

My word is my bond, is the old City code, but I never heard from him again.

So, I sought access to the email correspondences between Better Capital and the Irish Treasury, the latter of whom now discussed their part in the Fund through their Chief Legal Officer.

I also contacted the Irish politicians best known for their willingness to tackle disputes in public life; Dublin TD Shane Ross and Wexford TD Mick Wallace, both of whom expressed a desire to help.

The former advised of the forthcoming election and suggested, correctly, that he might have more power then, while Mick Wallace said that he had visited the Wikileaks founder, Julian Assange, under house arrest at the Ecuadorian Embassy in London. But without sight of the emails, he advised, it was my word against Moulton's. For a brief, fanciful moment, the thought of Assange made me wonder;

Could I hack the Irish Treasury?

After my representations to the Irish Prime Minister, nothing material was forthcoming from Better Capital nor the Treasury's Chief Legal Officer. It was another conflict, another battle in life that felt very much like David v Goliath. It felt like I was being stonewalled.

Six years later, a decade after the *Great Recession* began, I was still living with the effects of my second near-death experience, my financial one, but once again I had resolved to live.

Two decades had passed since I had made my *million-dollar* journey from *John Street to Wall Street*, and I was now on my longest losing streak, ever. But I had a family to support and life must go on, because it must. And I had my book to write.

EPILOGUE

Dad: I have seldom used the word Dad. When my elder sisters talked about Dad taking them to piano lessons or suchlike, it made me uncomfortable. I have always referred to him as 'my father' and for most of the eighteen years writing this story referred to him as Father; until a very recent edit. I rationalise this by acknowledging that somehow, I didn't feel that I'd had a dad.

Mum: In the years after Dad's death, Mum worked herself to death. In earlier drafts I have talked about her watching the early-evening sitcom, *Crossroads*, before returning to what was a daily night and day shift at the pub. In the story I refer to Martin and Paul reading book tomes, something I struggle to manage. I rationalise this by judging that when my time came, there was no time for books at bedtime.

Orphan: On Easter Sunday, April 5, 2015, I was staying at the Silverbirch Hotel, where I had boxed forty-years before at the time of Mum's death. I would return to London later that day, after attending the Tyrone v Kerry match at the nearby Healy Park. As I awaited lunch in the huge dining room, I felt strangely embarrassed to be among the large family groups by whom I was surrounded. At fifty-two-years of age, I was reminded of how it felt to be an orphan.

Nephew: As I left Healy Park after a hard-fought Kerry win over Tyrone, I met my nephew Stephen and his wife's uncle as they left their seats behind me. He was wearing a beanie hat to cover his chemo-induced bald scalp. He had been fighting cancer for ten years since he was a Masters student at Queen's University and died nearly four months later. He is survived by Julie, their three children, my sister Marie, and four siblings.

Reconciliation: Around that time, I was a chaplaincy visitor at Feltham Prison, London, meeting and greeting the young offenders before and after Catholic mass at the prison. 'Why are you here?' I said to one likeable young man. 'I just go a bit crazy on booze on Saturday nights,' he replied. After that, the chaplain arranged for me to speak with a group of church-going prisoners, that did not include my 'likeable young man', whom I hoped had been released. I sat in front of maybe ten youths, showed them my injuries, and told them about the hurt of my relationship with Paul, who had passed eight years before. One youth left while I was still talking about my crash, injuries, and rehabilitation, while another who I understood to be from the Irish Traveller community, promised to reconnect with a brother with whom he had not talked in years.

Life or Death: Recently while walking in Gunnersbury Park, West London, a swan flopped into a bush beside me while another landed on a steel fence. The male in the tree fell to the ground and was fine, but his mate appeared to have trapped her wing between the iron railings. I tried to lift her off the fence, but she was too heavy and pecked at me. I then realised that my right hand was covered in blood, so I got underneath her body and yanked her up into the air. I ran for help and found myself surprisingly distressed. She lost a wing and will spend the rest of her life in a swan sanctuary. The incident reminded me that but for the bravery of a young nurse, in my smoking car, I would not be writing these words.

Anniversaries: As I put the final words to T*he Million Dollar Irishman* story, I am reminded of the many anniversaries that coincided with my writing. When I first wrote about Mum's death, I realised that it was the fourteenth anniversary of my own near-death. The last words of that draft were written on Paddy's tenth anniversary, and recent returns from my editor coincided with Paul's thirteenth anniversary and Martin's thirty-third. Over the years, I have become prouder and prouder of this memoir, and right now, I feel privileged to have been the source of it all. It is as if they guided me to the end.

ACKNOWLEDGEMENTS

Family: To my sisters, Marie, Briegie, and Joanie, and especially Noelle at the time of the crash and ever since. To Niamh's parents, Tom and Angela for their love and family holidays.

Readers: To Paul Devlin and Noel McGinn who have read this story almost as many times as the author. To David Mackay and Terry Melia for fabulous support and encouragement during the final 'lockdown' edit. To Mike DeNardo for his wise counsel re Merrill. To Mickey Harte for his kind Foreward.

Editors: To Rowan Fortune who whipped the story into shape and was always available and insightful. To Vicky Blunden who helped me produce a manuscript to be proud of.

Book and Audio Launch: To James and Richard Keane, Your Publishing Solutions, for their tireless commitment and digital expertise with the eBook, Paperback and Audiobook. To my audiobook reader Colm Gormley, RSC, and Antoine Collin, Recording Engineer, for their excellent work at Bush Studios, London, for Audible. And to Alex Wade, Reviewed & Cleared, for the timely legal read and Gareth Graham, PFM, for the necessary insurance.

Literary consultant: To Vanessa Fox O'Loughlin, Inkwell Writers and Writing.ie, for believing in my story over many years, and for guiding me towards Simon and Declan, Gill Hess PR Agency, and Andrew Brown, Design for Writers.

Friends: To the late Pete Deighton for his great friendship and desire to see *The Million Dollar Irishman* story written. To Michael Bourke for his ongoing faith and to Aidan Bresnahan and Stephen Kee for their walk-on parts in the memoir. And to John McKinney, the great Omagh leader whose friendship I continue to treasure.

Omagh 1950's – Courthose at top of hill and Townhall beyond post on right

Licensee name, hand painted by Packie Quinn after Dad's death in 1966

Mum and Dad circa 1956

Me with friend Paul Martin – circa 1968

Glamour Boy, Paul, centre middle,
Confirmation, aged 10, 1972

Kates Bar football team, Harp Cup winners, Omagh Showgrounds, far right, circa 1983

Me, pageboy at Aunt Eileen's wedding, aged 5, 1968

Copy of front and back of Omagh Fund CD, summer 1999

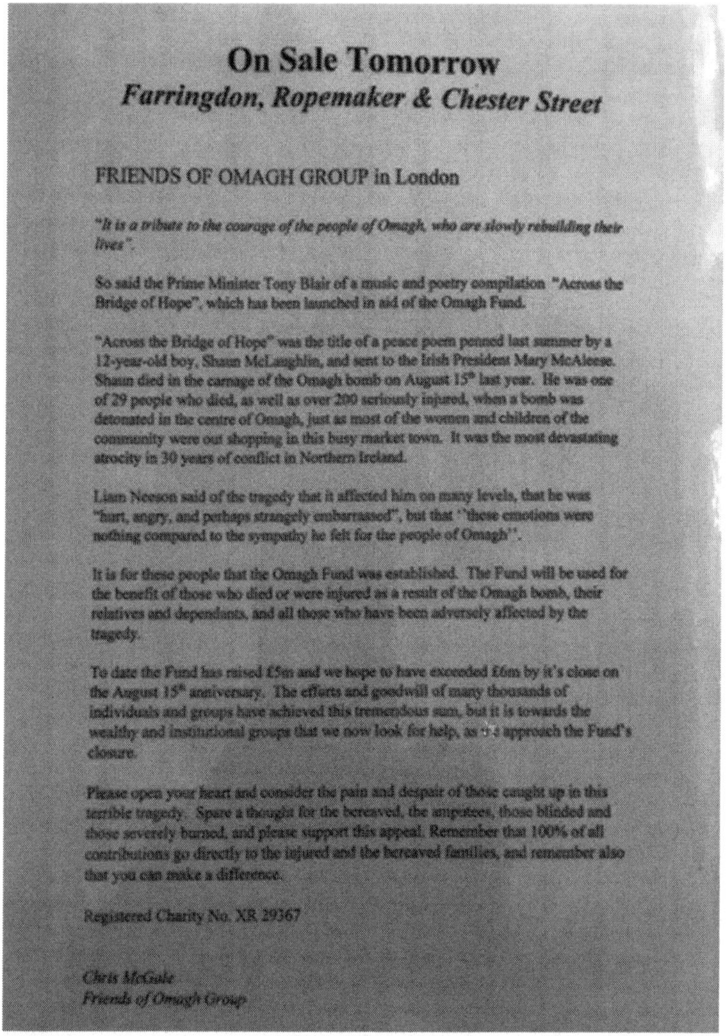

On Sale Tomorrow

Farringdon, Ropemaker & Chester Street

FRIENDS OF OMAGH GROUP in London

"It is a tribute to the courage of the people of Omagh, who are slowly rebuilding their lives".

So said the Prime Minister Tony Blair of a music and poetry compilation "Across the Bridge of Hope", which has been launched in aid of the Omagh Fund.

"Across the Bridge of Hope" was the title of a peace poem penned last summer by a 12-year-old boy, Shaun McLaughlin, and sent to the Irish President Mary McAleese. Shaun died in the carnage of the Omagh bomb on August 15th last year. He was one of 29 people who died, as well as over 200 seriously injured, when a bomb was detonated in the centre of Omagh, just as most of the women and children of the community were out shopping in this busy market town. It was the most devastating atrocity in 30 years of conflict in Northern Ireland.

Liam Neeson said of the tragedy that it affected him on many levels, that he was "hurt, angry, and perhaps strangely embarrassed", but that ''these emotions were nothing compared to the sympathy he felt for the people of Omagh''.

It is for these people that the Omagh Fund was established. The Fund will be used for the benefit of those who died or were injured as a result of the Omagh bomb, their relatives and dependants, and all those who have been adversely affected by the tragedy.

To date the Fund has raised £5m and we hope to have exceeded £6m by it's close on the August 15th anniversary. The efforts and goodwill of many thousands of individuals and groups have achieved this tremendous sum, but it is towards the wealthy and institutional groups that we now look for help, as we approach the Fund's closure.

Please open your heart and consider the pain and despair of those caught up in this terrible tragedy. Spare a thought for the bereaved, the amputees, those blinded and those severely burned, and please support this appeal. Remember that 100% of all contributions go directly to the injured and the bereaved families, and remember also that you can make a difference.

Registered Charity No. XR 29367

Chris McGale
Friends of Omagh Group

Note to colleagues re CD sale at Merrill Lynch offices, summer 1999

In Newmarket Winner's Enclosure, with Fairy Monarch – July 2001

Third from left with Joanie, Noelle on right,
Tyrone Players and Sam Maguire Cup - 2005

Evening Standard

SPORT BUSINESS CULTURE INSIDER THE ESCAPIST THE REVELLER COMMENT

Jon Moulton faces more misery as banker Chris McGale demands a €1 million fee

London *Evening Standard* – article by Michael Bow, October 09, 2015

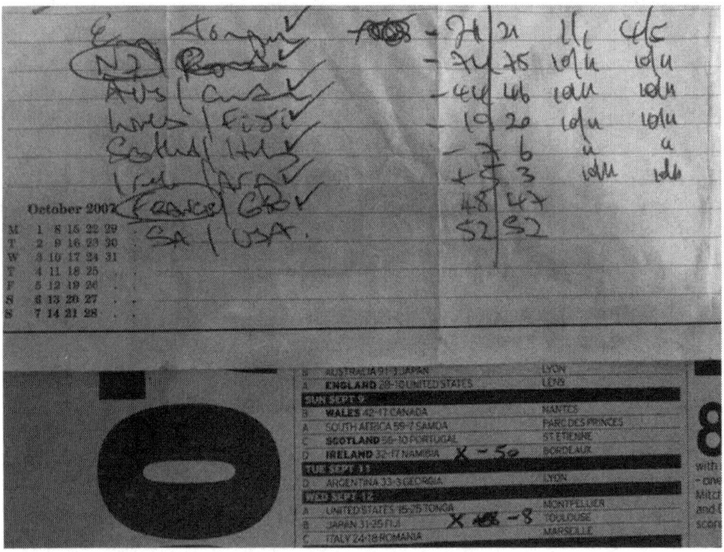

Betting extracts – Rugby World Cup, 2007

Life or Death: One-winged swan at
The Swan Sanctuary, 2020

Hoey's DAF truck, 1988 – from Dundalk Circuit Court file showing right-side impact